Way Ahead

A FOUNDATION COURSE IN ENGLISH

Workbook 5

MARY BOWEN   PRINTHA ELLIS

First published 1998 by
MACMILLAN EDUCATION LTD
London and Oxford
Companies and representatives throughout the world

ISBN 0–333–66158–3

10 9 8 7 6 5
07 06 05 04 03 02 01 00

Printed in Egypt by Zamzam Presses

A catalogue record for this book is available from the British Library.

Designed by Dave Glover

Illustrations by Thelma Cooper

Cover design and illustration by Wheeler and Porter

1

1 Write the names.

______ ______ ______ ______ ______ ______

2 Draw lines.

The Gordons 

The Gordons	is the youngest child.
Alex	is an old lady.
Joe	like their new house.
Sally	is interested in computers.
Their new neighbour	has a canary and a cat.

3 Correct the sentences.

The Gordons' new house is in Sun Street. ______

They are moving into number 22. ______

The house does not have a garden. ______

The Gordons have four pets. ______

Joe plays the violin. ______

Sally's cat is called Fin. ______

1 Read and write.

Ben, Tom and Sam are friends.

Sam is interested in reading. Ben plays the guitar.

Two of the boys like sports. One likes basketball and one likes swimming.

The boy who likes reading plays basketball.

Two of the boys have pets. One has a cat and the other has a canary.

The boy who plays the guitar is interested in computers but he does not like sports.

One of the boys is interested in photography. This boy has a cat, too.

The boy who likes reading does not have any pets.

	Ben	Tom	Sam
Hobbies:	________ ________	________ ________	________ ________
Pets	________	________	________

2 Make questions with ***have*** and ***like***. Write answers.

________ he ________ photography?
________ a camera?

Yes, ________ .
____

________ they ________ any pets?
What ________ ?

____
They ________
____

What about you?
________ many hobbies?
What sports ________ ?

____
I ________

1 Read and write the words.

1 The baby is sitting on her ____________ .

2 Look at the ____________ on that hat.

3 The cat is very ____________ the bird.

4 There is a swing on the ____________ .

5 A gorilla has a big ____________ .

6 The chair is going to ____________ .

7 He is not fat. He is ____________ .

2 Choose the right words.

loud, quiet, slow, quick, pretty

loudly, quietly, slowly, quickly, prettily

He plays the piano ____________ .

A horse runs ___________ but a snail is a very ___________ animal

Sshh! Stop crying! Be ____________ !

She has a nice voice. She sings very ____________ .

What a terrible noise. Please play more ____________ !

1 Number the pictures in order.

2 Write the story.

Use the past simple of these verbs:

break	give	fall	jump	see	put

1 Yesterday John ______________________________ .

2 ______________________________ in a vase.

3 ______________________________ .

4 ______________________________ .

5 ______________________________ off the table.

6 ______________________________ . What a mess!

3 Make questions.

What ______________________________ his mother? A bunch of flowers.

Where ______________________________ ? In a vase.

______________________________ on the floor? Yes, it did.

4 Correct the sentences. Use ***did not***.

John gave his mother a book. John did not give his mother a book. He gave her some flowers.

The cat saw a mouse. ______________________________

The dog jumped on the table. ______________________________

The table broke. ______________________________

Dictionary skills

1 **Match.**

suitcase guitar canary feather branch moon

2 **Write the words in ABC order.**

____

____

____

____

____

____

3 **Spelling.**
What is the difference?

stand - standing jump - jumping paint - painting	have - having take - taking give - giving

Write the verbs.

Mum is ________________ a cake. (make)

The babies are ________________ . (sleep)

My uncle is ________________ in America now. (live)

The Gordons are ________________ into a new house. (move)

Alex is ________________ his computer. (carry)

Joe is ________________ an old bike. (ride).

Composition

1 **Read.**

This is Joe Gordon. He is eleven. He has a brother called Alex and a sister called Sally. Alex is thirteen and Sally is twelve.

Joe has some hobbies. He is interested in music and he likes playing the guitar. He plays basketball and he is good at swimming, too.

Joe doesn't have any pets.

2 **Work with a friend.**
Ask questions and make notes.

... name?

How old ...?

... any brothers or sisters?

What ... called?

How old ...?

... hobbies?

... pets?

3 **Write about your friend.**
Draw a picture of him or her.

2

1 **Write the missing words.**

This woman comes from __ [ ] __ __ __ . 

If you go to New York, you will see this __ __ __ __ __ [ ] . 

Kangaroos come from __ __ __ __ __ __ __ [ ] __ . 

The pyramids are in __ [ ] __ __ __ . 

These people live at the __ __ __ __ [ ] Pole. 

This is a Chinese __ __ [ ] __ __ __ __ __ . 

This animal is a __ __ __ __ [ ] __ 

Penguins live at the __ __ [ ] __ __ Pole. 

This is African __ __ __ __ __ __ __ [ ] __ . 

The letters in boxes make a new word.
What is the word?

Miss Walker lives next door to Sally and Joe.

She is their [ ] [ ] [ ] [ ] [ ] [ ] [ ] [ ] [ ]

2 **Look at the souvenirs. Write.**

Has John been to America? ______________________________ .

Has Rose visited England? ______________________________ .

Where has Rose been? ______________________________ .

How many countries has John visited? ______________________________ .

Which countries have you visited? ______________________________ .

1 Where have they been?
Look and finish the sentences.

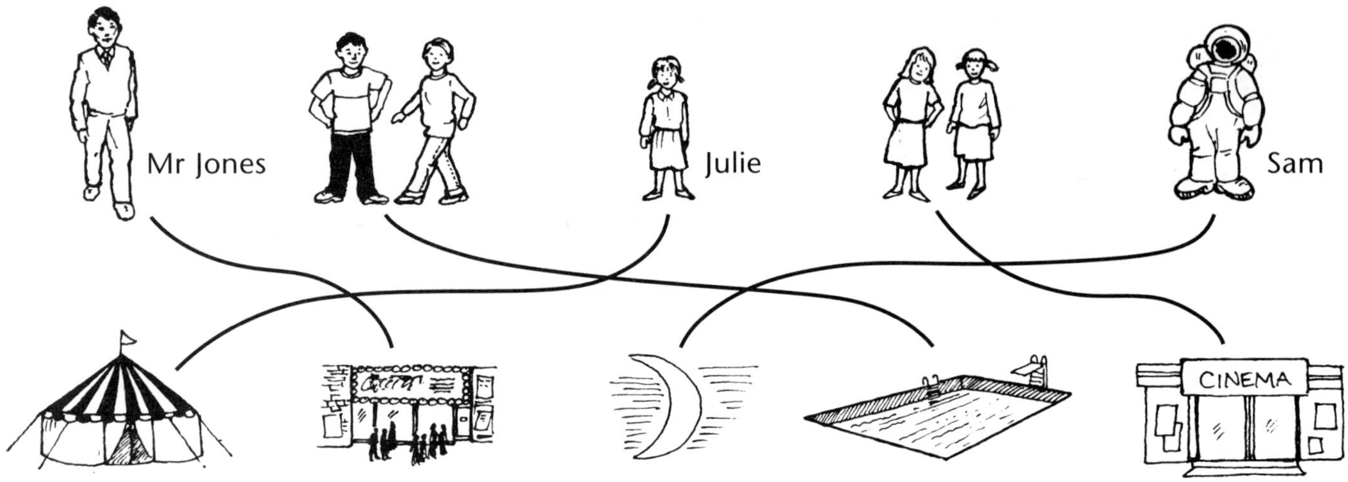

Mr Jones has been to the theatre.

The boys ______________________________ .

Julie ______________________________ .

The girls ______________________________ .

Sam ______________________________ .

2 What is Rose asking John?
Write the questions. Use these verbs:

climb	ride	see	make

Have you ever ______________________________ ?

______________________________ ?

______________________________ ?

______________________________ ?

3 Write *ever* or *never*.

Have you __________ been to London?

No, I haven't.
I've __________ been there.

Has John __________ travelled by plane?

No, __________ .

Rosie has __________ swum in the sea. Have you __________ swum in the sea?

1 Who are they?
Finish the sentences.

A person who travels is a ______________________________ .

A person who writes is a ______________________________ .

A person who drives is a ______________________________ .

A teacher is a person who ______________________________ .

A typist is ______________________________ .

A student ______________________________ .

2 Countries and languages.
Finish the sentences.

They speak Turkish in ______________________________ .

They speak Chinese in ______________________________ .

In America they speak ______________________________ .

In Morocco they speak ______________________________ .

They speak Russian in ______________________________ .

3 Imagine you are a traveller.
Think and write about a journey you have made.

Was your journey long or short? ______________________________

______________________________ .

Where did you go? ______________________________

______________________________ .

How did you travel? ______________________________

______________________________ .

What did you see? ______________________________

______________________________ .

Were you happy or sad to come home? ______________________________

______________________________ .

1 Read.

Last year Max went to America. He travelled by plane. He stayed in New York for one week. He liked it very much. He saw the Statue of Liberty, he took lots of photographs and he bought nice presents for his friends at home.

Write questions about Max.

Where did ______________________________ ? To America.

____ ? By plane.

____ ? For one week.

____ ? Yes, he did. Very much.

____ ? The Statue of Liberty.

____ ? Yes, he did. Lots.

____ ? Nice presents.

2 Read again about Max. Write about Kate.

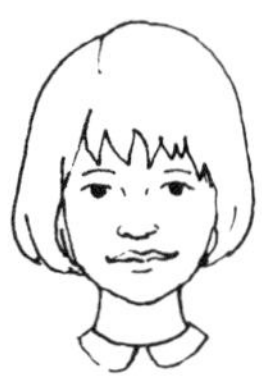

1996 Kate → Egypt

Cairo two weeks

____

____

____

____

____

Dictionary skills

You are reading. You see a word which you do not understand. What do you do?
Do you open your dictionary? NO! Don't open your dictionary yet. THINK!
You know something about this word and you can guess.

1 **Look! What do you think the underlined words mean?**

My mother went to the baker's and bought four pink meringues.
a) animals? b) hats? c) cakes?

After working hard all day, I felt exhausted.
a) happy? b) tired? c) sad?

The teacher was delighted when the children gave her flowers.
a) unhappy? b) hungry? c) happy?

The train was going to leave so John rushed to the station.
a) hurried? b) walked? c) cycled?

Jenny looked inside the box and shrieked with fright.
a) fell over? b) made a frightened noise? c) laughed?

2 **Spelling.**
What is the difference?

walk - walked	play - played
rain - raining	snow - snowing

stop - stopped	hop - hopped
run - running	swim - swimming

Write the verbs.

The girl is ________________ on the floor. (sit)

The children ________________ TV yesterday. (watch)

It ________________ last night. (rain)

Mum is ________________ Sally's hair. (cut)

The boys are ________________ football. (play)

Yesterday the bus ________________ outside the school. (stop)

Composition

1 **Read this postcard.**

Dear Joe,

We are having a very bad time here. The food in the hotel is terrible and the weather is wet and windy. We have swum in the swimming pool. The water is very cold. I have ridden a horse, too. Have you ever ridden a horse?

See you soon,

Don

ADDRESS

Mr Joe Smith
48 Hunter Street
London
England

2 **Write a postcard to a friend. Write about a good holiday.**

Use these words:

hot and sunny	camel	sea
good	delicious	warm

ADDRESS

3

1 **Write a verb under each picture.**

cleaning	playing	sleeping	painting	helping	driving

____

____

____

____

____

____

2 **Finish the sentences.**
What were they doing at 4 o'clock yesterday?

At 4 o'clock Jim was ______________________________ .

Ken ______________________________ .

Molly ______________________________ .

The cats ______________________________ .

Miss Jones ______________________________ .

The boys ______________________________ .

What were you doing at 4 o'clock yesterday?

______________________________ .

What were your friends doing?

______________________________ .

1 Look and write.

Today   Yesterday

Today she ______________________.

Yesterday ______________________.

______________________.

Yesterday ______________________.

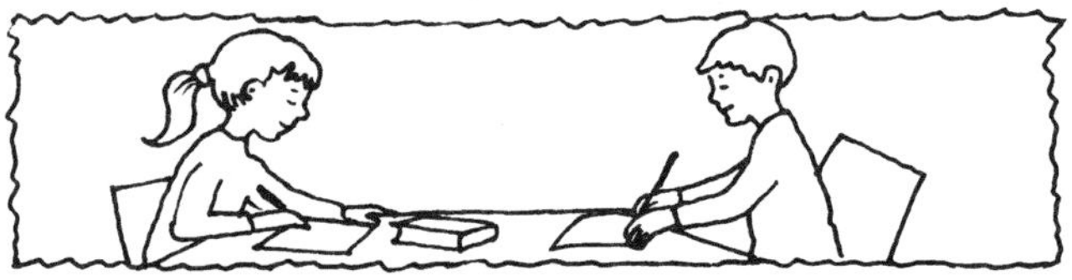

______________________.

______________________.

Today I ______________________.

Yesterday ______________________.

2 Look and write.
What were they doing?

While mum ______________________, the twins ______________________.

While the boy ______________________, the girl ______________________.

While dad ______________________, mum ______________________.

1 Read, write and find the extra word.

England	backwards	the sun	
a watch	New York	the earth	a candle
a marble	space	an hour	east

Find …

two things which spin. ____________ ____________

two things which shine. ____________ ____________

the opposite of west. ____________

a country in Europe. ____________

a city in America. ____________

something which tells the time. ____________

a word which means 60 minutes. ____________

What is the extra word? ____________

Draw a picture.

2 Read and write the letters.

A	B	R	U
A	G	A	U
L	C	I	N
start here	E	T	S

Travel north 2 squares …
Walk east 3 squares …
Go south 2 squares …
Go west 1 square …
Walk north 3 squares …
Travel west 2 squares …
Travel south 2 squares …
Go east 2 squares …
Walk north 1 square.

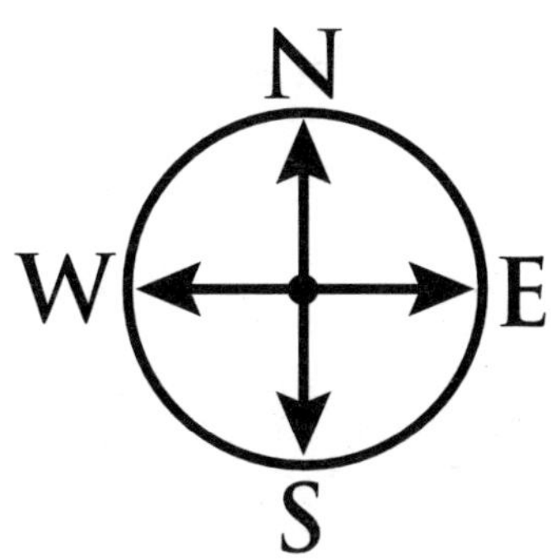

Where are you?

___ ___ ___ ___ ___ ___ ___ ___ ___

1 **Look at this!**

Read.

What is wrong?

Underline the mistakes and then correct them.

It is seven o'clock in New York and two o'clock in Moscow. While the American children are getting up, the Russian children are eating their lunch.

____

It is twelve o'clock in London and ten o'clock in Sydney. While the Australian children are eating their lunch, the English children are going to bed.

____

While the Chinese children are eating their dinner, the Russian children are having lessons at school. It is eight o'clock in Moscow and two o'clock in Beijing.

____

2 **Write about the children.**

New York / Sydney — While the children in New York are ____________________

the children in Sydney ________________________ .

London / Beijing ________________________________

____

Moscow / New York ________________________________

____

Dictionary skills

1 **Look at these pages from a dictionary.**

There are words at the top of each page. They show the first word and the last word on two facing pages.

Point to the words. What are they?

A

mislay

mislay (mɪsˈleɪ) *vt* lose (something) for a short time, esp. by forgetting where it is.

mislead (mɪsˈli:d) *vt* give incorrect information or advice to (someone).

misled (mɪsˈled) past tense and past participle of **mislead.**

mismanagement (mɪsˈmænɪdʒmənt) *nu* failure to handle the affairs of a business, etc., well.

misplace (mɪsˈpleɪs) *vt* **1** direct (one's confidence, enthusiasm, etc.) towards an unworthy object. **2** put (something) in the

take. ● *vt* **1** be wrong about (something): *We have mistaken our way.* **2** (followed by **for**) suppose (someone or something) to be (someone or something else): *I mistook you for your sister.* **mistaken** (mɪsˈteɪkən) past participle of **mistake.** ● *adj* **1** wrong; in error: *He was mistaken about her age.* **2** wrongly supposed: *mistaken identity.* **3** unwise: *In a mood of mistaken jealousy she sent him away.*

mistletoe (ˈmɪsəltəʊ) *nu* a plant with small white berries that grows on various trees in

molest

and water don't mix. **4** meet people: *One should try to mix at a party.* ● *nc infml* See **mixture. mixed** *adj* **1** made by mixing. **2** for people of both sexes, different races, etc.: *a mixed school; mixed sport.* **mixer** *nc* a machine for mixing food, cement, etc. **a good** or **bad mixer** a person who gets on well or badly with all kinds of people. **mixture** (ˈmɪkstʃə*) *nc* also **mix** a combination of different elements; blend; variety. **mix up 1** confuse: *I mix him up with his brother.* **2** involve: *mixed up in crime.*

moderate (ˈmɒdərɪt) *adj* **1** medium; neither strong nor weak, etc. **2** (of opinions, etc.) reasonable; not extreme. ● *nc* a person with moderate political views. ●(ˈmɒdəreɪt) *vti* (cause to) become moderate: *You ought to moderate your drinking.* **moderately** *adv* **moderation** (ˌmɒdəˈreɪʃən) *nu* the state of being moderate; reasonableness.

modern (ˈmɒdən) *adj* **1** to do with the present or the recent past. **2** of the time since the end of the Middle Ages (about 1500).

B

mollusc

mollusc (ˈmɒləsk) *nc* one of a class of animals with shells and soft bodies, including snails and oysters.

molt (məʊlt) *US v, n* See **moult.**

molten (ˈməʊltən) *adj* **1** (of metals, etc.) melted; liquid. **2** made from melted metal.

moment (ˈməʊmənt) **1** *nc* a very short time. **2** *nu* importance. **at the moment** just now; at present. **for the moment** for now; for the present. **the moment** as soon as: *The moment he comes, you can go.* **momentary** (ˈməʊməntərɪ) *adj* lasting only a moment.

monochrome (ˈmɒnəkrəʊm) *nu, adj* **1** (of paintings, printing, etc.) (in) one colour. **2** (of films, television, etc.) black and white.

monogamy (məˈnɒgəmɪ) *nu* marriage to one wife or husband at a time.

monogram (ˈmɒnəgræm) *nc* a pattern made from two or more letters, usually the first letters of a person's names, and used to ornament handkerchiefs, etc.

monologue (ˈmɒnəlɒg) *theatre nc* **1** a long speech by one actor in a play. **2** a piece written for only one actor to speak.

mortar

mood[1] (mu:d) *nc* a state of mind or feeling. **moody** *adj* **-ier, -iest** (of a person) **1** whose state of mind or feeling varies a lot. **2** bad-tempered.

mood[2] *grammar nc* any of the classes into which verbs are divided according to whether they express statements, wishes, orders, etc.

moon (mu:n) **1** *nc* a planet that moves around a larger planet. *nu* **2** the moon that goes around Earth. **3** the moon as seen from Earth: *There will be a full moon to-*

morality (məˈrælɪtɪ) **1** *nc, pl* **-ties** a system of morals. **2** *nu* rightness.

morass (məˈræs) *nc* a bog; stretch of muddy land.

morbid (ˈmɔ:bɪd) *adj* **1** diseased; to do with disease: *a morbid growth.* **2** unusually concerned with death: *morbid thoughts.*

more (mɔ:*) *determiner, pron* **1** a larger quantity (of): *I have more books than you.* **2** a further quantity (of): *Would you like some more?* ● *adv* **1** (used to form comparatives) to a greater degree: *The town is more*

C

mortgage

mortgage (ˈmɔ:gɪdʒ) *nc* a loan made to a person so that he can buy a house, the house being the security for the loan. ● *vt* offer (a house) as security for a loan of money.

mortify (ˈmɔ:tɪfaɪ) *vt* make (someone) feel shame: *He was mortified by her dislike of him.*

mortuary (ˈmɔ:tjʊərɪ) *nc, pl* **-ries** also **morgue** a place where dead bodies are kept before being buried.

mosaic (məˈzeɪɪk) *nc* a picture or pattern

(a machine or chain of events). **motionless** (ˈməʊʃənlɪs) *adj* completely still; not moving. **motion-picture** *nc* a film for the cinema.

motivate (ˈməʊtɪveɪt) *vt* provide (someone) with a motive; encourage. **motivation** (ˌməʊtɪˈveɪʃən) *nu*

motive (ˈməʊtɪv) *nc* a reason (for an action). ● *adj* causing motion; that makes someone act: *motive force.*

motley (ˈmɒtlɪ) *adj* **1** mixed; varied: *a motley crowd of people.* **2** of many colours.

muck

moulding *US* **molding** (ˈməʊldɪŋ) **1** *nu* shaping, influencing. **2** *nc* a piece of shaped wood or stone on or around a door, etc.

moult *US* **molt** (məʊlt) *vi* (of some birds and animals) lose its feathers, skin, etc. ● *nc* the process of losing feathers or skin.

mound (maʊnd) *nc* **1** a very small hill. **2** a bank of earth or stones built as a protection. **3** *infml* a huge heap: *a mound of papers to be read.*

mount[1] (maʊnt) *vt* **1** get up onto (a horse, etc.). **2** climb or go up (stairs, a hill, etc.). **3**

of a bay, etc. ● (maʊð) *vt* move one's mouth to make (words) but without speaking. **mouthful** *nc* **1** the amount of food a person can chew and swallow comfortably at a time. **2** *infml* a long and complicated word. **mouthpiece** (ˈmaʊθpi:s) *nc* **1** the part of a musical instrument, etc., which the player or user puts to or into his mouth. **2** a person who speaks for an organisation.

movable (ˈmu:vəbəl) *adj* able to be moved. **movable feast** one of the important dates in the Christian calendar that occur on a

2 **Where would you find these words?**
Write A, B or C.

money ______ mitten ______ moss ______ moat ______

mop ______ moth ______ much ______ moccasin ______

monsoon ______ mole ______ moose ______ mount ______

Composition

1 **Look at this!**

2 **Think about these questions.**

Where did Jim go yesterday? Where did he sit and who did he look at?
What was a little girl building?
Was her brother helping her? What was he doing?
Where was their mother sitting?
How many people were swimming? Were they having fun?
What was the weather like? Was the sun shining?

3 **Now write about the picture.**

4

1

Draw lines.
What do these animals give us?

leather | milk | eggs | wool | meat

Write about the animals.

From sheep we get ________________ , ________________ and ________________ .

____

____

____

2

Finish the sentences.
What was happening yesterday at Hilltop Farm?
Choose words from both boxes.

visit	show around	work
play	swim	milk

the cows	on the pond	in the barn
in the dairy	the farm	visitors

Joe and Sally were ____ .

The farmer ____ .

The farmer's wife ____ .

Colin ____ .

The lambs ____ .

The ducks ____ .

1 Read and match.

If you go to the farm,	if he is not careful.
If you visit the dairy,	Colin will show you around.
If you look on the pond,	if they go on the school trip.
You will see the lambs	you will meet the farmer's wife.
The goats will eat Joe's hat	you will see the ducks.
The children will have fun	if you look in the barn.

2 Complete the sentences.

If the sun ______________________, we ______________________ to the beach. (shine, go)

We _______________ not _______________ if the water _______________ cold. (swim, be)

If the children _______________ good, Mum _______________ them ice creams. (be, buy)

We _______________ all day if the weather _______________ fine. (stay, be)

3 What about you? Finish the sentences.

If the weather is fine this weekend, ____ .

I will help my mum and dad if ____ .

If I finish my homework quickly today, ____ .

I will go to bed early if ____ .

1 Match the animals with their young.

lamb calf duckling foal kid chick

2 Find the words.

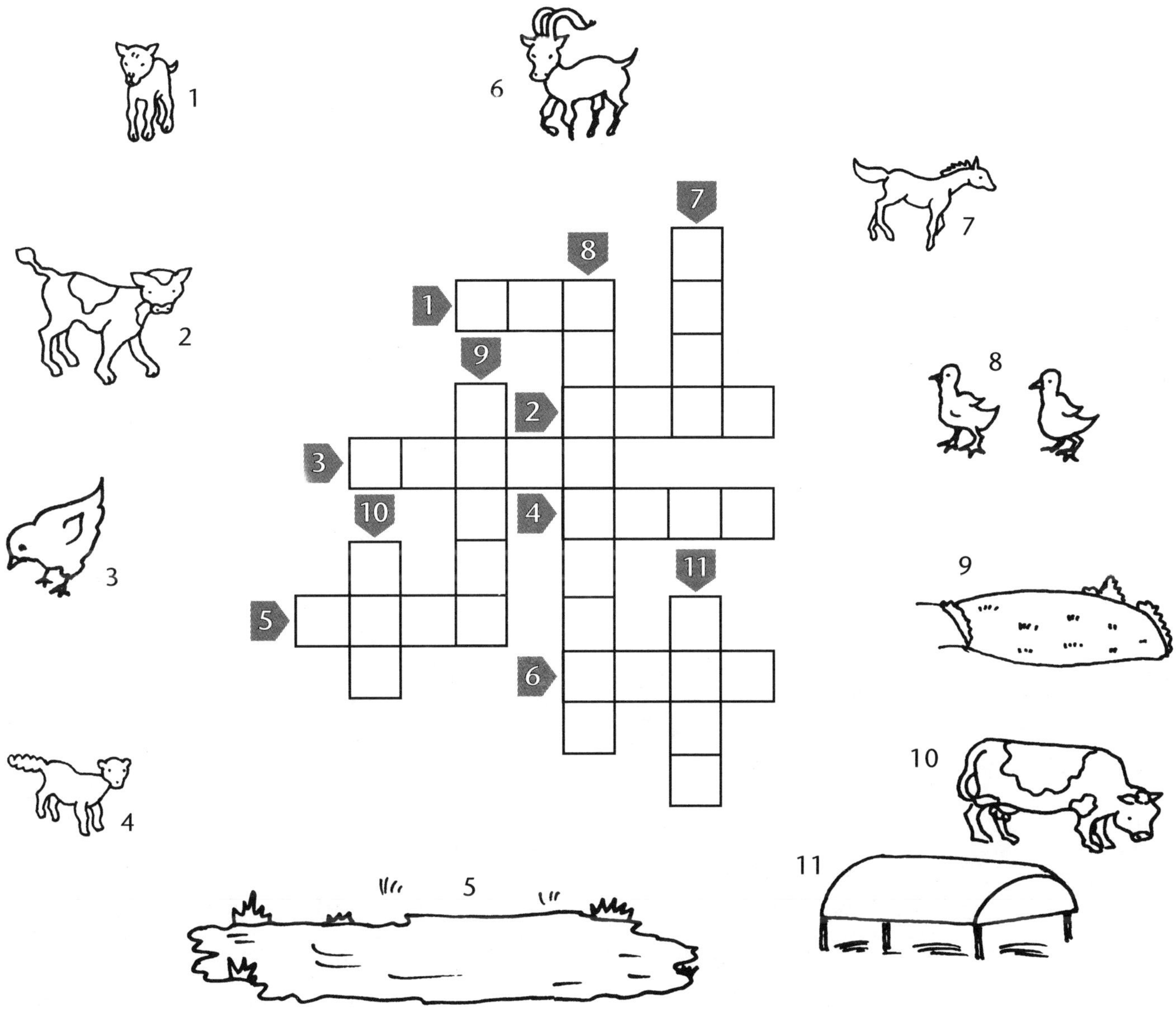

1 Complete the sentences.

Use these words: myself yourself himself herself

Where did you go yesterday?

I went to the circus.

Did you enjoy ____________ ?

Yes, I enjoyed __________ very much.

I went to the beach but I did not enjoy ___________ at all.

Why didn't you enjoy ___________?

Because the weather was cold.

2 Look and write.

Ben went to the theatre and he enjoyed himself.

Maggie ____.

Ted ______________________ but ______________________.

Sandy ____.

Mike ____.

Dictionary skills

1

Finding nouns.

A noun is the name of a person, an animal, a thing or a place.

Look at the underlined words. They are nouns.

The man rode his horse very fast along the road.

John and his sister went to America by plane.

My aunt bought a kilo of apples, a chicken and some cheese.

2

Underline the nouns in these sentences.

Two girls came out of the house carrying a large, heavy box.

The kitten jumped onto the table and knocked over a glass of milk.

Henry and his mother went to London by train.

3

Abbreviations.

In a dictionary the abbreviation for a noun is *n*.
(You may also see *nc*, *nu*, *ncu* and *n pl*)

Look at this page.

How many nouns can you find? Circle them.

bed

beach (biːtʃ) *nc* land, esp. sand, at the edge of the sea. ● *vt* run or pull (a boat) onto a beach. **beachhead** ('biːtʃhed) *nc* land near the sea occupied by soldiers who have arrived in boats to attack.

beacon ('biːkən) *nc* a bright light which can be seen from far away and acts as a guide or signal.

bead (biːd) *nc* a small piece of glass, coloured stone, etc., a number of which can be put on a string and worn round the neck as an ornament. **2** a drop, esp. of sweat.

beady ('biːdɪ) *adj* **-ier, -iest** (esp. of the eyes) round and hard in appearance.

beagle ('biːgəl) *nc* a kind of dog.

beak (biːk) *nc* the horny mouth of a bird.

beaker ('biːkə*) *nc* **1** a tall cup without a handle. **2** a tall glass container with a lip, used in scientific experiments.

beam (biːm) *nc* **1** a piece of wood that goes across a room and helps to support the ceiling or the roof. **2** a light that shines straight from the sun or a lamp. **3** a broad smile. ● *vi* **1** shine brightly. **2** smile broadly. **3** *vt* direct (a broadcast) towards a particular place.

bean (biːn) *nc* **1** any of several plants of which the seeds are eaten as vegetables. **2** one of these seeds. **full of beans** very energetic. **one's bearings** find out or forget where one is or the direction one wants to go in. **ball bearing** See under **ball[1]**.

beast (biːst) *nc* **1** an animal, esp. one with four feet. **2** a cruel or dirty person. **beastly** ('biːstlɪ) *adj* **-ier, -iest 1** like a beast. **2** nasty.

beat (biːt) *nc* **1** a sound that is repeated regularly, as of a drum or the heart. **2** a rhythm in music. **3** a conductor's movements indicating this to the musicians. **4** a way regularly walked by someone such as a policeman. ● *vt* **1** hit repeatedly. **2** stir (food) fast and thoroughly. **3** defeat. **4** *vi* (esp. of the heart) make regular movements that can be heard. **beat about the bush** avoid an important matter by not talking about it plainly. **beat off** win the fight against (an attack, etc.). **beat up** knock (someone) about violently. **beating** ('biːtɪŋ) *nc* **1** repeated hits. **2** a defeat.

beaten ('biːtən) past participle of **beat.** ● *adj* **1** (shaped by being) hit repeatedly: *beaten metal.* **2** (of food) mixed thoroughly: *beaten egg.* **3** defeated. **off the beaten track** away from big towns and main roads.

beater ('biːtə*) *nc* a person who makes birds fly up so that they can be shot.

Composition

1 **Talk about the pictures.**
The questions will help you.

<u>Lindy's day at the farm.</u>

What did Lindy visit last week?
Did she go with her family or her class?

What did they see first?
What was the farmer doing?

Where was the farmer's wife?
What was she making?

What did they see in the field and on the pond?

What did they like inside the barn?
What did they like outside?

Were there lots of animals on the farm?
Did Lindy enjoy herself?

2 **Now write about Lindy.**

5

1 **Find the words and write.**
Where are they going on Saturday?

Jane ______________________ .

Pete and Dan ______________________ .

Ann and Kay ______________________ .

Ricky ______________________ .

Mr and Mrs Sims ______________________ .

2 **Look and write.**
What are they doing at the weekend?

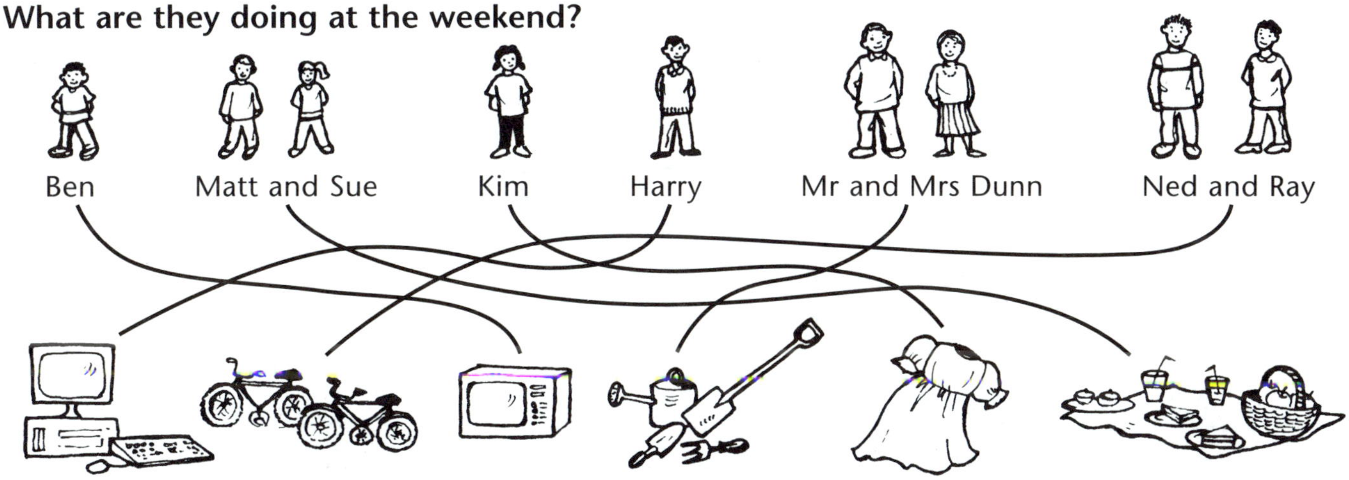

Use these verbs: ride work buy play have watch

____

____

____

____

____

____

1 Look at this.

Ann's diary	
Mon	study
Tues	Maths test
Wed	
Thur	shopping – new shoes!
Fri	visit Grandma
Sat	tennis with Sue
Sun	help Mum

Paul's diary	
Mon	basketball
Tues	Maths test
Wed	shopping – new trainers
Thurs	swimming
Fri	
Sat	football match with Dad
Sun	cinema

2 Right or wrong?
Write ✔ or ✘.

Paul is going swimming on Wednesday.

Paul is watching a football match on Saturday.

Ann is visiting her grandma on Sunday.

They are having a maths test on Thursday.

They are going shopping next week.

Ann is helping her mum on Tuesday.

3 Correct the wrong sentences. Use *not*.

____

____

____

____

4 Make questions.

Ann - study - Monday? Is Ann studying on Monday?

Paul - football match - Sunday? ______________________

Ann and Paul - maths test - Tuesday? ______________________

When - Ann - mother? ______________________

What - Paul - Monday? ______________________

Dictionary skills

1 **Finding verbs.**

A verb tells you what happens (the action) in a sentence.
What does a noun *do*? The verb tells you.

Look at the underlined words. They are verbs.

The ball bounced across the road.

The train had left the station before we arrived.

A dog started to bark as the man entered the house.

2 **Underline the verbs in these sentences.**

The sun was shining on the sea.

When she got home, my sister baked a cake.

John wanted to buy a bike but it was too expensive.

3 **Abbreviations.**

In a dictionary the abbreviation for a verb is *v*.
(You may also see *vi, vt* and *vti.*)

Look at this page.

How many verbs can you find? Circle them.

four round pieces on a board marked out in thirty-two white, and thirty-two black squares. **draughtsman** ('drɑːftsmən) *nc, pl* **-men** **1** a draftsman. **2** one of the round pieces in the game of draughts.

draw (drɔː) *vt* **1** pull, esp. using some effort; move by pulling: *a horse drawing a cart; Draw the curtains.* **2** pull up or out: *draw water from a well; have a tooth drawn.* **3** *vti* make pictures, figures, lines, etc., with a pencil, etc.; give a picture of in words. **4** *vt* attract the attention, interest, etc., of: *The procession drew huge crowds.* **5** *vti* end (a game) without either side having won. **6** *vi* move forward, close, etc.: *They drew near to the town.* ●*nc* **1** a game that ends without either side having won. **2** *nu* taking by chance: *the luck of the draw.* **drawback** ('drɔːbæk) *nc* something that delays or gets in the way of progress; disadvantage. **drawbridge** ('drɔːbrɪdʒ) *nc* a bridge that can be pulled up to stop people crossing or in order to let ships pass. **draw in** **1** (of daylight) get shorter: *The nights are drawing in.* **2** encourage to join in: *He was drawn into their conversation.* **3** arrive and stop: *The train drew in at the station.* **draw out** **1** (of

thing happens) while asleep. **2** imagine (something) while awake. **not dream of** not consider: *I wouldn't dream of going.* **dreamer** *nc* **1** a person who dreams. **2** person who has hopes, plans, etc., that are not likely to come true. **dreamy** *adj* **-ier, -iest** **1** having hopes, plans, etc., that are not likely to come true. **2** like a dream; not real: *dreamy music.*

dreamt (drempt) past tense and past participle of **dream.**

drear ('drɪə*) *literary adj* sad; gloomy.

dreary ('drɪərɪ) *adj* **-ier, -iest** dull; without happiness or comfort; sad: *dreary weather.* **drearily** ('drɪərɪlɪ) *adv*

dredge (dredʒ) *v* **dredge up** bring up (mud or pieces of plants or rocks), from the bottom of a river or sea. ●*nc* a device for doing this work.

dregs (dregz) *n pl* **1** the waste bits remaining at the bottom of a liquid. **2** the part that is useless and worst: *the dregs of humanity.*

drench (drentʃ) *vt* make thoroughly wet: *We got drenched in the heavy rain.*

dress (dres) **1** *vti* (cause to) have clothes on: *Are you dressed yet?* *vt* **2** put a bandage, etc., on (an injury): *dress wounds.* **3** make

Composition

1 **Look at this.**

Tom's week

Mon	dentist
Tues	–
Wed	basketball with Ben
Thurs	shopping with mum – new trainers
Fri	–
Sat	visiting grandpa – lunch
Sun	cinema with Joe

On Monday I am going to the dentist. On Tuesday I am not doing anything. On Wednesday I am playing basketball with my friend Ben. He's very good at basketball. On Thursday I am going shopping with my mother. I want to buy some new trainers. I am not doing anything on Friday. On Saturday I am visiting my grandfather. We are having lunch with him. On Sunday I am going to the cinema with my friend Joe.

2 **Now you!**

Mon	____________________
Tues	____________________
Wed	____________________
Thurs	____________________
Fri	____________________
Sat	____________________
Sun	____________________

3 **Write about your week. Add details if you want.**

____

____

____

____

____

____

____

Revision

1 **Choose the correct verbs.**

have	play	live	like	know

The Gordons __________ in Moon Street. The children __________ a lot of hobbies. Alex __________ a lot about computers. Joe __________ the guitar. Sally __________ a cat but Joe __________ not __________ a pet. The children __________ basketball and tennis but their parents __________ not __________ sports.

2 **Write the verbs.**

Yesterday John __________ to the cinema. He __________ a good film. (go, see)

It __________ Sue's birthday last week. Her mother __________ her a cake. (be, make)

Sue's father __________ her a watch and her brother __________ her a book. (buy, give)

Last night a picture __________ from the wall and __________ on the floor. (fall, break)

3 **Make questions.**

________ you ever ________ to China?	Yes, I have.
When ______________________ there?	Last year.
______________________________?	Yes, I enjoyed myself very much.
__________ ever __________ a panda?	Yes, I have. I saw one last week.
Where ______________________ it ?	I saw it in the zoo!
What ______________________ ?	It was sleeping.

4 Finish the sentences.
What were they doing at 2 o'clock yesterday?

Colin ______________________________.

James and Jack ______________________________.

Laura ______________________________.

I ______________________________.

We ______________________________.

5 Write negative sentences. Use ***not***.

John was playing.  No. He ______________________________.

Jane bought a parrot.  No. ______________________________.

I have been to China.  No. I ______________________________.

They have apples.  No. ______________________________.

We are working tomorrow.  No. We ______________________________.

6 Finish the sentences.

We'll go to the beach if ______________________________.

If it rains, I ______________________________.

If you go to the zoo, ______________________________.

He will go to the doctor if ______________________________.

They will be late if ____________ not ______________________________.

6

1 Write questions.

seen  What has the dog just seen ?

had  ________ the cat ________ ?

broken  ________ the girls ________ ?

made  ________ the boys ________ ?

taken  ________ the man ________ ?

Write the answers to the questions. Use *just*.

The dog ________ .

The cat ________ .

The girls ________ .

The boys ________ .

The man ________ .

3 Read and match.

You need a camera 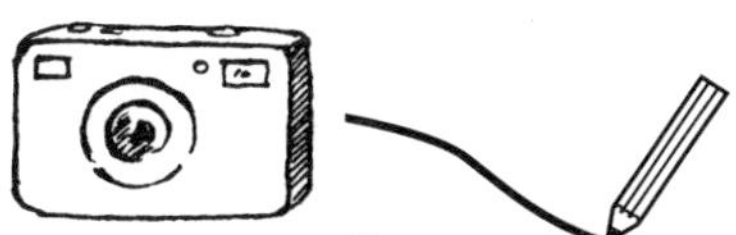 for cycling.

You need brushes  for sewing.

You need boots  for cooking.

You need a helmet  for taking photos.

You need an apron  for painting.

You need a needle and thread  for playing football.

1 Write the past participles.

take ____________ make ____________

do ____________ climb ____________

ride ____________ jump ____________

play ____________ see ____________

find ____________ break ____________

have ____________ finish ____________

done	found	seen
played	broken	jumped
had	ridden	made
climbed	finished	taken

2 Complete the sentences. Use *just*.

She has just finished the book.

I ____________________ this watch in the street!

We ____________________ a snowman!

The horse ____________________ over the fence.

She ____________________ a camel.

They ____________________ the mountain.

3 Find the word.

Can you name these things? Take the first letter of each word. The letters make a new word.

What has Mandy just found?

She ____

Can you draw it?

1 Find the hobbies.

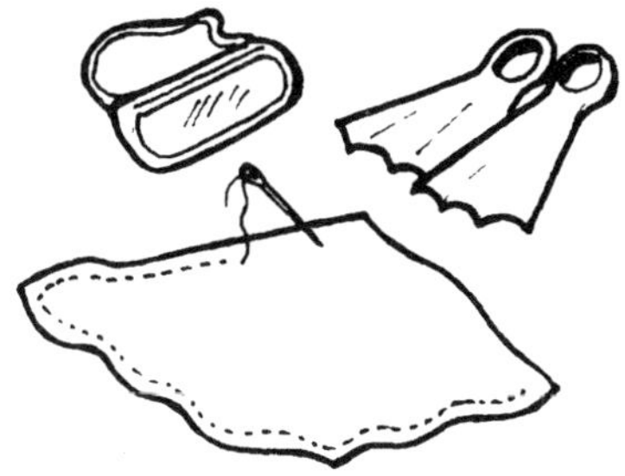

L	B	V	I	O	L	I	N	D	U	M	X	T
O	A	K	R	E	A	D	I	N	G	F	Y	L
P	M	P	O	S	T	C	A	R	D	S	A	B
G	W	O	F	C	Y	C	L	I	N	G	N	T
S	E	W	I	N	G	B	T	E	N	N	I	S
H	S	T	A	M	P	S	C	P	I	A	N	O
S	W	I	M	M	I	N	G	D	O	L	L	S
E	P	A	I	N	T	I	N	G	G	E	H	L
V	T	R	Q	U	G	U	I	T	A	R	I	M

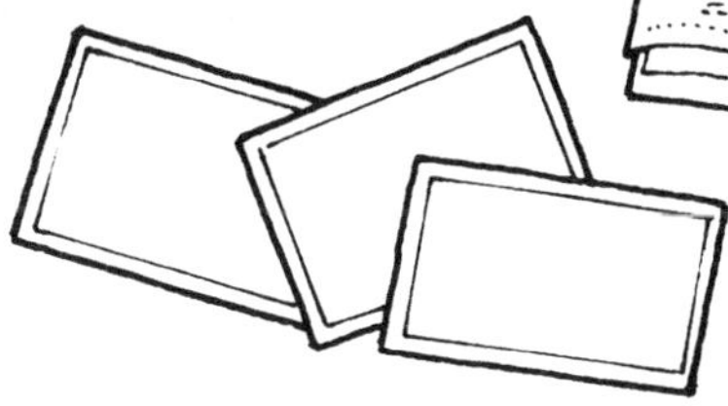

2 Put the hobbies in groups.

sports	collecting	music	other hobbies
________	________	________	________
________	________	________	________
________	________	________	________

3 What is wrong? Use *too*.

The guitar ______________________________ .

The bike ______________________________ .

She has ______________________________ .

She plays ______________________________ .

1 **Read.**

When Jenny was very small, she liked playing with her mother's chess set. She liked the chess pieces because they were pretty. Her favourite pieces were the kings, the queens, the horses and the castles. When she was five, her mother taught her how to play.

Jenny plays chess with her mother and her friends. She cannot play with her sister because she is not old enough. She does not like playing with her brother because he is not good enough. She has just played a game with him and she has won – again!

2 **Write the answers.**

Why did Jenny like her mother's chess set? ______________________ .

When did she learn to play? ______________________ .

Does she play well or badly? ______________________ .

Why can't she play with her sister? ______________________ .

Who has she just played a game with? ______________________ .

Who has won? Why? ______________________ .

3 **Finish the sentences. Use *not* ... *enough*.**

She can't carry the suitcase because she is not strong enough. .

You can't swim because the water ______________________ .

He can't play chess because he ______________________ .

I can't play basketball because I ______________________ .

I can't wear these shoes because they ______________________ .

Don't eat those strawberries. They ______________________ .

Dictionary skills

1 Match.

camel clock chips crown cup corner

2 Write the words in ABC order.

____

____

____

____

____

____

3 Spelling.

Look, listen and write.

Is the underlined sound long or short? Write L or SH.

apple

bubble

table

bottle

needle

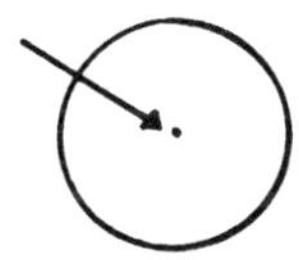
middle

________ ________ ________ ________ ________ ________

Cover and write.

____

____

____

____

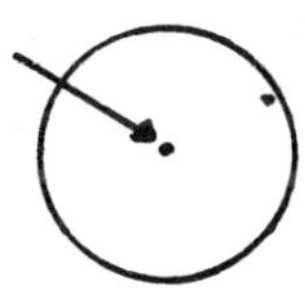
____

____

Composition

1 **Look at this.**

I like playing football.

I like collecting stamps.

I like playing the piano.

2 **Think of questions you can ask the children about their hobbies.**

3 **Ask your friends about their hobbies. Make notes.**
Write about their hobbies and your hobby too.

Our hobbies

7

1 What are the words?

Alex is a very good ________________ .

He has taken some interesting ________________ .

One of them has just won a ________________ .

It is a photo of his ________________ .

Today Alex is speaking to a ________________ .

Alex has won a nice ________________ .

It is a ________________ .

gapohertorph

hopsot

tiponomceti

bigenhoru

perroret

zerip

marcae

2 Read and match.

Alex has taken …

He has just won …

He has been interested in photography …

He has known Miss Walker …

He has had his new camera …

for a short time.

since yesterday.

some good photos.

a photography competition.

for about two years.

3 Complete the sentences.

Alex is very interested ________ computers.

Miss Walker has travelled all ________ the world.

Joe is good ________ basketball.

A new camera was Alex's prize ________ winning the competition.

A reporter wrote a story ________ Alex.

1 Write *for* or *since*.

Miss Walker has lived in her house ________ thirty years.

Alex has had his camera ________ yesterday.

The Gordons have known Miss Walker ________ a short time.

Sally has been in the garden ________ two hours.

Joe has not played basketball ________ August.

The children have not seen their cousins ________ last summer.

2 Write the sentences.

Alex - have - computer - a year

Alex has had his computer for a year.

Joe - play - guitar - six months

____.

The Gordons - live - Moon Street - September

____.

We - be - friends - a long time

____.

I - have - not - see - the cat - yesterday

____.

Miss Walker - know - the Gordons - six weeks

____.

Mr Gordon - have - car - last year

____.

1 Choose present perfect or past.

The girls ______________________________ table tennis together for nine months. (play)

Pat ______________________________ the team in July. (join)

The Bridge Street boys ________________ just ________________ another match. (win)

They ________________ only ________________ three games since December. (lose)

Paul ______________________________ interested in poetry for several years. (be)

Last year he ______________________________ a poem called 'The Beach'. (write)

2 Read and write.

Paul Morton's poem, 'The Beach', won first prize in a poetry competition.
Can you write his poem?

on the blue sea	the grey waves crash and	those hot summer days.	
and children laugh and play	A lonely seabird calls	the bright sun sparkles	
Were they a dream?	high in the icy air.	on the golden sand.	the wind bites.

In summer ____________________________

____

____

____

____

But in winter ___________________________

____

____

____

____

It is hard to remember ____________________

____

____

1 Find the past participles.

fallen	taken	broken	grown	blown	found

grow ____________ blow ____________ take ____________

break ____________ fall ____________ find ____________

2 Write.

Look at the TV news. What has happened?

____

____

____

____

____

____

3 Write the questions.

A reporter is talking to Kelly, one of the table tennis players from West Hill School.
What are his questions? Use these words:

Why?	When?	What?	How often?	How long?	How many?

______________________________? I started playing two years ago.

______________________________? I like it because it's a very fast game.

______________________________? I've been in the school team for nine months.

______________________________? We play three times a week.

______________________________? We haven't lost any matches.

______________________________? We've just won the Under 12 competition.

Dictionary skills

1

Finding adjectives.

An adjective is a word which describes a noun. An adjective tells you more about a noun.

Look at the underlined words. They are adjectives.

My brother is tall but my sister is short.

My favourite uncle has a new, red car.

The bright sun shone on the sparkling waves.

2

Underline the adjectives in these sentences.

A dangerous tiger was roaring in the dark jungle.

His jacket is new but his trousers are old.

Golden stars twinkled in the black sky.

3

Abbreviations.

In a dictionary the abbreviation for a adjective is *adj*.

Look at this page.

How many adjectives can you find? Circle them.

graze^2 *vti* touch or scratch (something, esp. the skin) lightly: *I grazed my knee on the ground; The bus was so wide it only just grazed past.* ● *nc* a place where something has been grazed: *Is that a graze on your knee?*

grease (gri:s) *nu* soft fat or soft, solid oil, used esp. to make machines work smoothly. ● *vt* put grease on. **greasy** *adj* **-ier, -iest**.

great^1 (greɪt) *adj* **-er, -est** 1 large in size or number. 2 lasting a long time; unusually long: *a great while; He lived to a great age.* 3 important: *a great change.* 4 very clever, able, etc.: *a great writer.* 5 keen: *a great stamp collector.* 6 *infml* good, enjoyable, etc.: *Have a great time!* **Great War** See **World War I** under **world**. **greatly** *adv* **greatness** *nu*

great^2 *adj* (used as a prefix to indicate a child of a grandchild, a parent of a grandparent, or an aunt or uncle of a father or mother): *great-grandchildren; a great-grandfather.*

greed (gri:d) *nu* wanting too much of something, esp. food. **greedy** *adj* **-ier, -iest.**

green (gri:n) *adj* **-er, -est** 1 of the colour of, for example, growing grass. 2 looking ill, esp. seasick. 3 not having had much experience. 4 (of fruit) not yet ripe. 5 (of meat) not smoked or cured: *green ham.* ● *ncu* 1 grey. **grey matter** 1 the grey, active parts of the brain. 2 *infml, humorous* the brain.

grid (grɪd) *nc* 1 a set of crossing lines, drawn, for example, over a map. 2 a system of pipes or wires by which gas, water, or electricity is fed around a country.

griddle (ˈgrɪdəl) *nc* 1 a flat metal plate for cooking on. 2 a type of wire net for separating large stones, etc., from small ones.

grief (gri:f) *nu* great sadness, esp. at someone's death. **come to grief** meet with failure, an accident, etc.

grievance (ˈgri:vəns) *nc* a real or imagined cause for complaining.

grieve (gri:v) *vti* (cause to) feel grief.

grievous (ˈgri:vəs) *adj* 1 very serious: *a grievous crime.* 2 causing grief.

grill (grɪl) *vt* 1 cook (food) by heating from just above or from just below. 2 *infml* question (someone) forcefully. ● *nc* 1 a device for grilling food. 2 a set of metal bars on which food is grilled. 3 a dish of grilled food. 4 a restaurant where grills are the main food served.

grille (also **grill**) (grɪl) *nc* 1 a set of metal bars fastened together in a pattern as a screen, etc. 2 also **radiator grille** a set of metal bars on the front of a car, lorry, etc., to let air flow to the engine.

grim (grɪm) *adj* **-mer, -mest** 1 cruel, forbidding, or merciless. 2 *infml* unpleasant or

Composition

1 **Look and read.**

Grandmother wins painting prize

Mrs Amy Banks – 80 years old – 16 grandchildren
1st prize in painting competition. Prize = holiday for 2 – Italy
started painting 6 months ago
favourites: family (grandchildren), friends, animals
winning painting: her cat – sleeping – garden. Title: Candy
Mrs B. – happy, excited. "It's wonderful! I've never been to Italy!"

2 **Think about these questions:**

How old is Mrs Amy Banks? How many grandchildren does she have?
What has she just won? What is her prize?
When did she start painting?
What does she like painting?
What is her winning painting called? Can you describe the painting?
How does Mrs Banks feel? What did she say?

3 **Write a short newspaper report about Mrs Banks.**

8

1 Draw lines and make the sentences.

Bread 	are mixed	together into dough.
If yeast	is kneaded	in the oven to bake.
The flour, yeast and water	are put	from flour, yeast and water.
The dough	is made	the bread will rise.
The loaves	is added	and cut into loaves.

2 Write the sentences.

Bread ____.

____.

____.

____.

____.

3 What's the word?

1 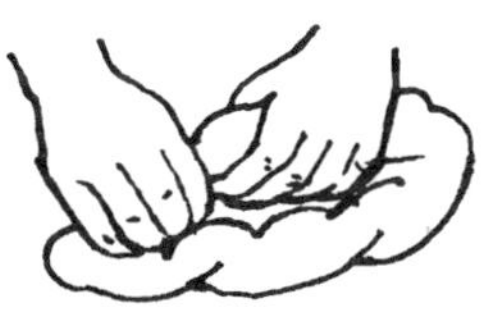

2 

3 

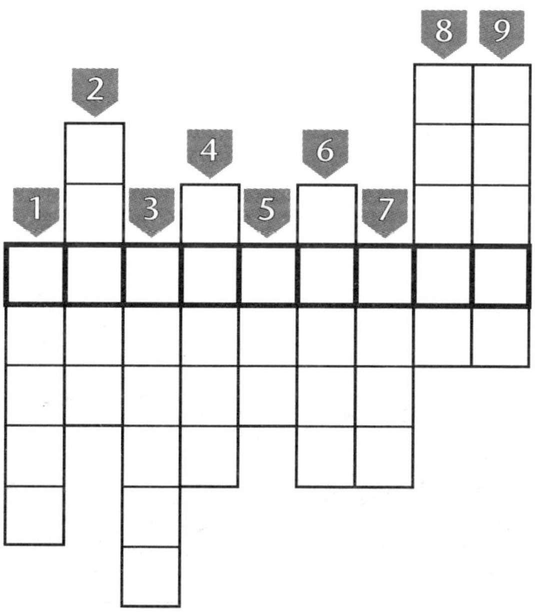

7 

8 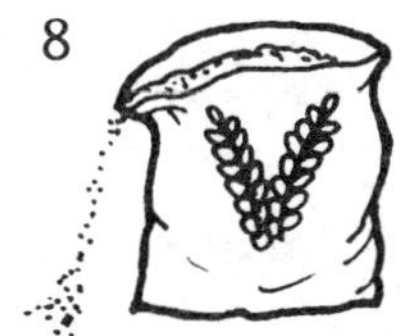

9 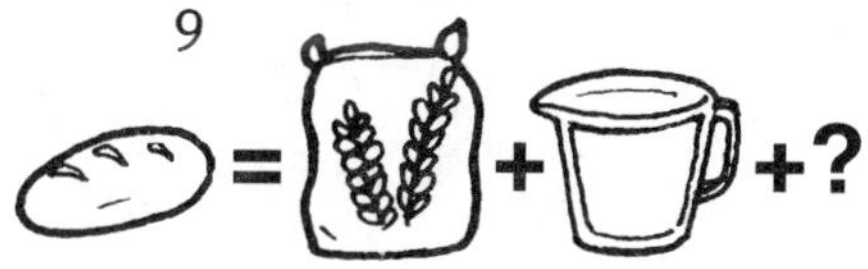

4 The flour is _________ with the water and yeast.

5 The dough is _________ into loaves.

6 If yeast is added, the bread _________ .

1 Write.
What are they made of?

It is made of wood.

They ______.

______.

______.

______.

______.

______.

2 Complete the sentences.

Bread is made at the bakery. (make)

Flour ______ with water and yeast. (mix)

The dough ______ into loaves. (cut)

The loaves ______ in an oven. (put)

Cakes ______ at the bakery, too. (sell)

Bread ______ all over the world. (eat)

3 True or false? Write ✔ or ✘.

Toys are always made of wood. ☐

Cakes are baked at a bakery. ☐

Meat is sold by the baker. ☐

Sweets are only eaten by children. ☐

Photos are taken with a camera. ☐

Poems are only written by girls. ☐

4 Correct the false sentences. Use *not*.

Toys are not ______.

______.

______.

______.

1 How is a pair of jeans made?

Look at the pictures.

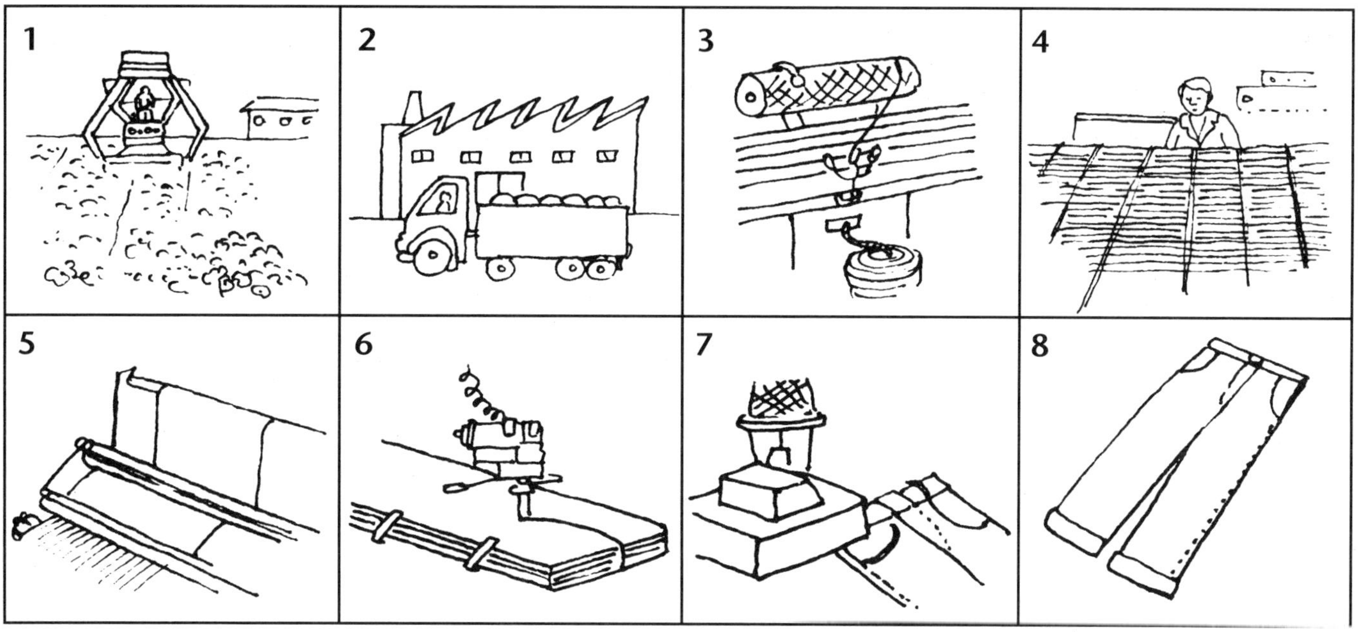

2 Complete the sentences using these words:

taken	sewn	made	cut	woven	dyed	picked

First the cotton is ________________ and then it ________________ to a factory. There it ________________ into yarn. The yarn ________________ blue and then it ________________ into cloth. The cloth ________________ and the pieces ________________

Look! A nice pair of jeans!

3 Write.

How many pairs can you see?

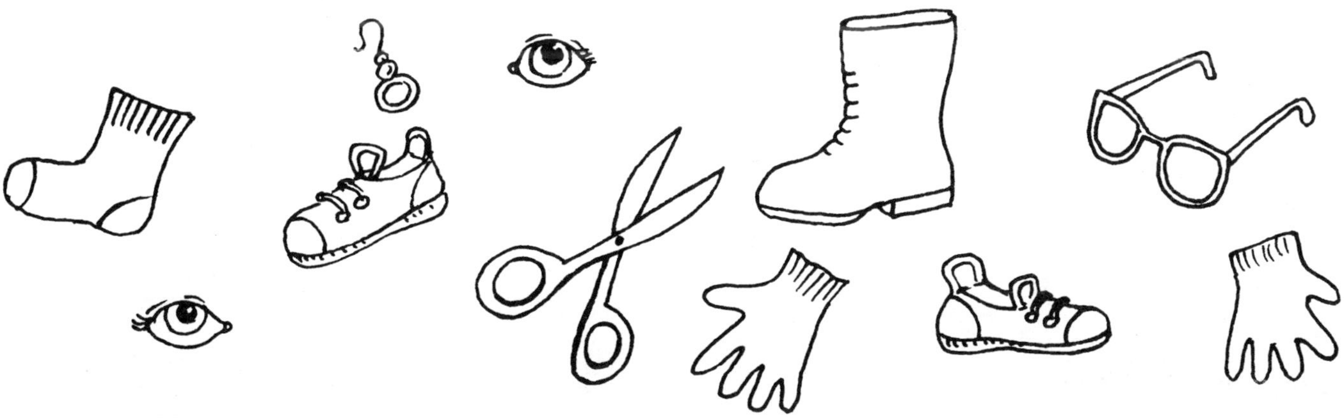

I can see ... a pair of ________________ ________________

________________ ________________

________________ ________________

1 Read and write the names.

Bob Snip and his brother, Ted, are tailors. They own a small tailor's shop and they make beautiful shirts. Their families help in the shop, too. Bob always cuts the cloth and his wife, Molly, pins the pieces together. Ted is good at sewing so he sews the pieces together with his old sewing-machine. Bob's daughter, Rose, sews on the buttons. Ted's wife, Nellie, irons the shirts and her son, Tom, picks up the pins from the floor.

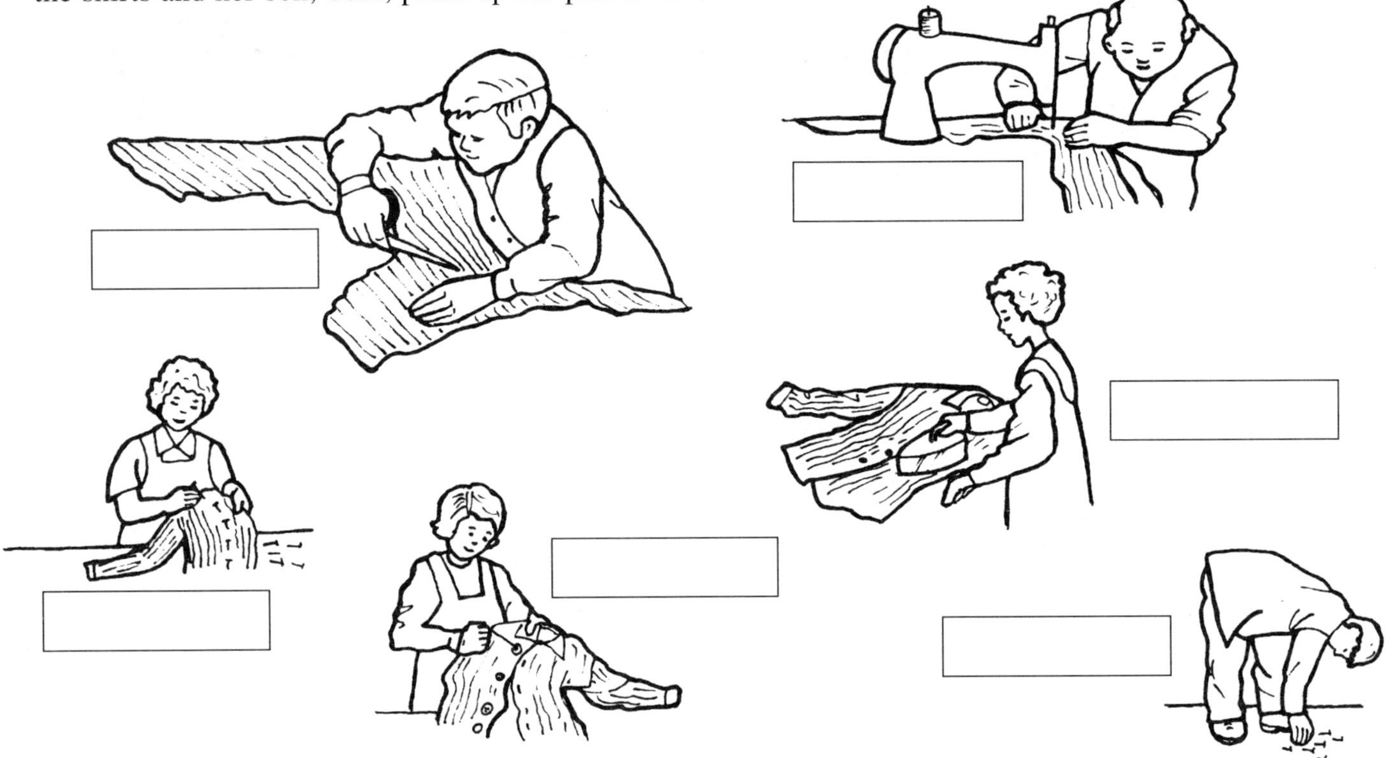

2 Look at the picture and answer the questions.

Like this:

Who owns the shop? The shop is owned by Bob and Ted.

Who cuts the cloth? ______________________.

Who pins the pieces together? ______________________.

Who sews the shirts? ______________________.

Who irons the shirts? ______________________.

Who sews on the buttons? ______________________.

Who picks up the pins? ______________________.

3 Can you say it?

Say this sentence as fast as you can.
Say it again and again!

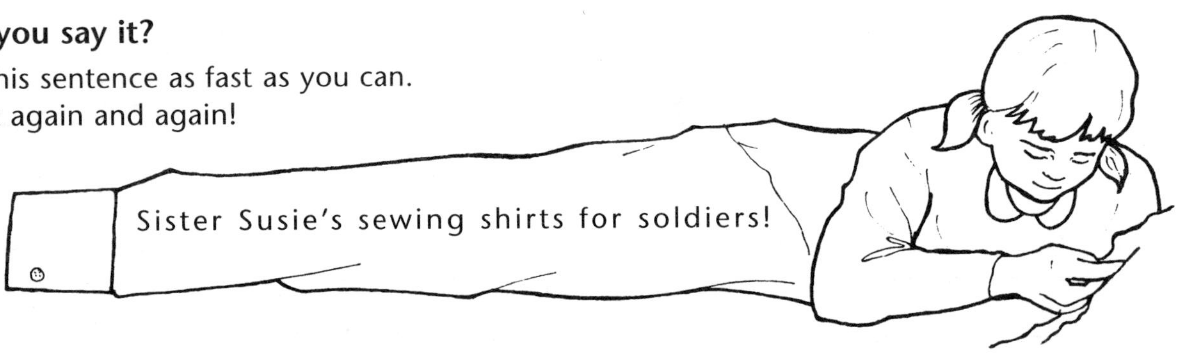

Dictionary skills

1 Finding adverbs.

An adverb tells you more about a verb. It answers the questions When?, Where? or How?

Look at the underlined words. They are adverbs.

Yesterday I could not sing loudly.

The horse jumped quickly over the fence and galloped home.

I play tennis well but I ride badly.

2 Underline the adverbs in these sentences.

My sister dances beautifully.

The children played quietly today.

He wanted to go fast but his bike was so old that he rode slowly.

3 Abbreviations.

In a dictionary the abbreviation for a adverb is *adv*.

Look at this page.

How many adverbs can you find? Circle them.

quarter. 4 *US* one fourth of a dollar; twenty-five cents. ● *vt* 1 divide into quarters. 2 provide (soldiers) with **quarters.** **quarter note** *music, US* See **crotchet. quarter past** or **to** fifteen minutes after or before (an hour in the day). **quarterly** (ˈkwɔːtəlɪ) *adj, adv* (happening, etc.) once every three months: *quarterly payments*. ● *nc, pl* **-lies** a paper, magazine, etc., that is printed and sold once every three months.

quarters (ˈkwɔːtəz) *n pl* a place for someone, esp. a soldier, to live in. **at close quarters** very near or close up: *It's not very pleasant, seen at close quarters.*

quartet (kwɔːˈtet) *nc* 1 a group of four singers or musicians. 2 a piece of music for such a group.

quartz (kwɔːts) *nu* a hard, shiny mineral found in many rocks.

quash (kwɒʃ) *vt* put an end to, esp. by the power of law.

quaver (ˈkweɪvə*) *vi* 1 speak or sing with a shaking voice. 2 (of music) tremble; shake. ● *nc* a musical note lasting half as long as a crotchet.

quay (kiː) *nc* a place to which ships are tied up for goods to be loaded or unloaded.

queen (kwiːn) *nc* 1 the wife of a king. 2 the woman ruler of a country. 3 a woman thought to be the best of a certain group: *a beauty queen*. 4 the playing-card in each suit carrying the picture of a queen.

queue (kjuː) *US* **line** *nc* a line of people, vehicles, etc., waiting to be served in a shop, continue their journey, etc. ● *vi* (often followed by **up**) form or wait in a queue.

quibble (ˈkwɪbəl) *vi* argue about or object to a small, unimportant thing, esp. to avoid a matter. ● *nc* such an argument or objection.

quick (kwɪk) *adj* **-er, -est** 1 (moving) fast; taking a short time. 2 thinking fast; eager: *a quick mind*. ● *adv infml* quickly. **quicken** (ˈkwɪkən) *vti* make or become quick or quicker. **quicklime** (ˈkwɪklaɪm) *nu* a white solid used in making steel, paper, etc. **quicksand** (ˈkwɪksænd) *nc* deep, wet sand that draws things down inside it. **quicksilver** (ˈkwɪkˌsɪlvə*) *nu* another name for mercury.

quiet (ˈkwaɪət) *adj* **-er, -est** 1 with little or no noise. 2 with little or no movement or disturbance; calm. 3 secret; private: *I'll have a quiet word with him.* ● *nu* the state of being quiet. **quietly** *adv* **quietness** *nu*

quill (kwɪl) *nc* 1 a whole, large feather from a bird's wing or tail. 2 such a feather made into a pen to write with. 3 one of the needle-like parts on the back of some animals, such as a hedgehog.

quilt (kwɪlt) *nc* a thick bed-covering made up of two layers filled with wool or feathers. **quilted** *adj* filled with soft material for warmth, comfort, etc.

Composition

Making biscuits

flour

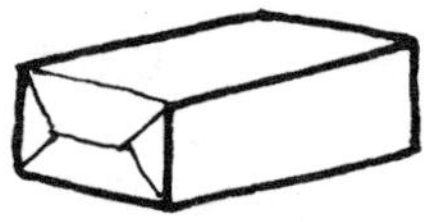
butter

sugar

1 **Look at the pictures and talk about them.**
The words under each picture can help you.

mixed together

added

dough - rolled out

cut into shapes

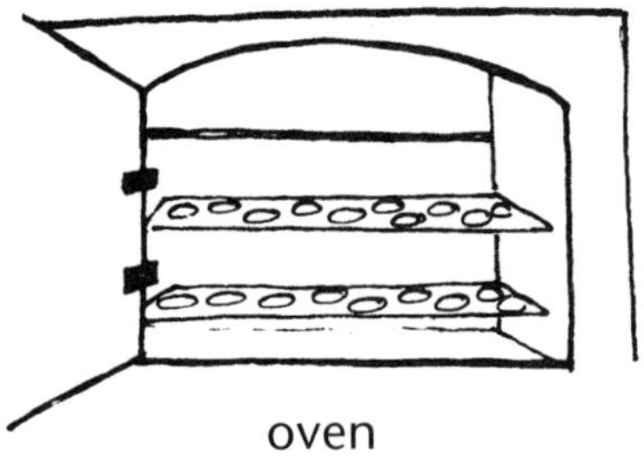
oven

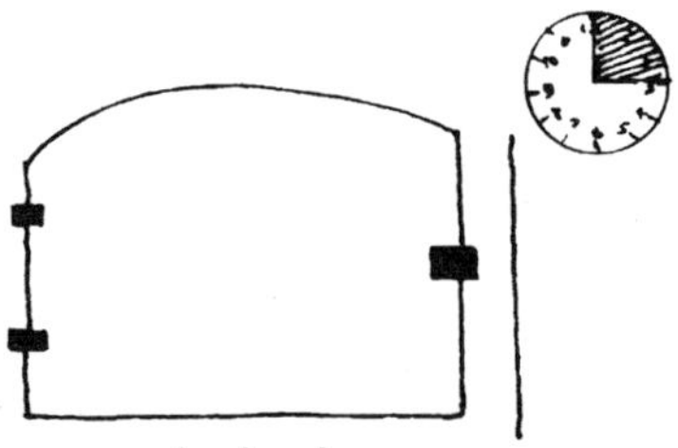
baked

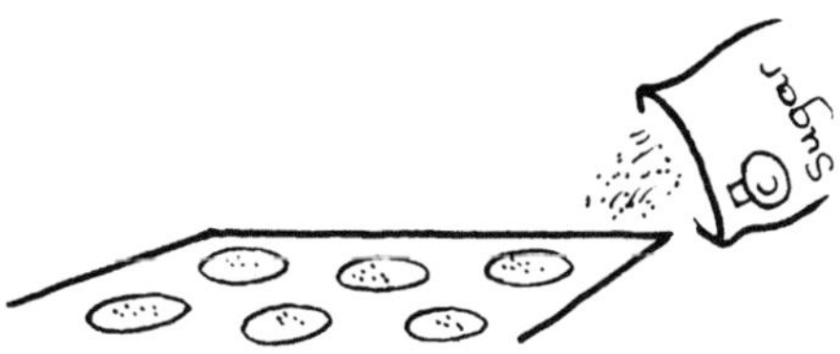

covered with

put

taken

2 **Write.**

First the butter and sugar ______________________________ .

Then ______________________________ .

After this ______________________________

and ______________________________ .

Then ______________________________

____

and ______________________________ .

Next ______________________________

and then ______________________________ .

9

1 Underline the mistakes.

Alex keeps five tropical fish in a small tank.
He has been spending a little of his money on them.
Alex wants to buy a cheap pet.
He has been saving his pocket money for a short time.
Sally and Mrs Gordon have been waiting in the sitting room.
Alex has bought a horse.

Write the sentences and correct the mistakes.

____

____

____

____

____

2 Answer the questions.

You and your pocket money.

Do you get pocket money? ______________________________

How often do you get pocket money? ______________________________

Who gives it to you? ______________________________

Do you save your pocket money? No ☐ Yes ☐

→ Are you saving for something at the moment? No ☐ Yes ☐

→ What is it? ______________________________

Do you like spending your pocket money? No ☐ Yes ☐

→ What do you spend your pocket money on?

____

1 Write the verbs.

play	wait	skate	shop	study

He has been waiting since 3 o'clock.

She ______________________ since 1995.

We ______________________ for two hours.

I ______________________ for ages.

They ______________________ for hours.

He ______________________ since April.

2 Make sentences.

I - learn English - five years

I have been learning English for five years.

The baby - sleep - twelve hours

____.

They - live in Moon Street - September

____.

I - play table tennis - 1994

____.

We - wait - this morning

____.

Alex - save - pocket money - ages

____.

1 Which one is different?

A  B  C  D 

D. The tie is different because it does not have stripes.

A  B  C  D 

____.

A  B  C 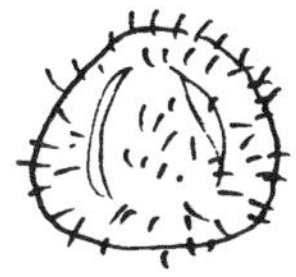 D 

____.

A  B  C  D 

____.

A  B  C  D 

____.

2 Answer the questions.

Why does a tiger have stripes?

It has stripes so that it can

Why does a polar bear have white fur?

____.

Why is a crocodile dark green?

____.

Why does a hedgehog have spines?

____.

Why does a tortoise have a hard shell?

____.

1 Write the questions.

Tony Bates works at the zoo. Sally is talking to him. What questions does she ask?

How long ______________________________ ?

I've been working here for five years.

Which animals ______________________________ ?

I look after the lions and the tigers.

______________________________ ?

I've been looking after them since last year.

______________________________ this morning?

I've been cleaning their cages.

______________________________ in this cage?

Yes, there is. She's lying on that big branch.
She's sleeping.

______________________________ ?

She's been sleeping there all the morning.

2 Look and write.

What have the animals been doing all morning?

eat hop sleep talk play swim

The tiger has been ______________________________ . ______________________________ .

______________________________ . ______________________________ .

______________________________ . ______________________________ .

Dictionary skills

1 **Match the words with their abbreviations.**

noun　　verb　　adjective　　adverb

adj　　*n*　　*adv*　　*v*

2 **Look at the underlined words in these sentences.**
Copy the words and write the abbreviations.

The <u>teacher</u> brought a <u>pet</u> to school. ____________________ ____________________

The dog <u>barked</u> <u>loudly</u>. ____________________ ____________________

<u>Happy</u> children <u>were playing</u>. ____________________ ____________________

He plays his <u>new</u> violin <u>well</u>. ____________________ ____________________

3 **Read the sentences and put the words in the right boxes.**

A pretty girl was sitting quietly under the big tree.

The black and white horse ran fast along the street.

There were delicious cakes and bread in the window of the small bakery.

The children played happily on the sandy beach.

nouns	**verbs**	**adjectives**	**adverbs**

Composition

1 **Read this letter from Alex to his penfriend Paul.**

37 Hill Street,
Newtown,
Devon EX35 8BT
17th March 1997

Dear Paul,

Thank you for your letter.

I am twelve years old and I live in Newtown. It is a small town.

We have been living here for three months.

My family is quite big. There is my mum, my dad, my grandma, my two sisters and my brother. We have three cats and a dog. Do you have any pets?

My hobbies are football, collecting stamps and playing the guitar. I have been playing the guitar for two years. At school my favourite subjects are maths and science. I like French, too. I have been learning it since January.

Please write soon. It is nice to have a penfriend.

From,

Alex

2 **Now you! Write a letter to a penfriend.**

Remember to write your address and the date. Write about your town, your family and pets, your hobbies and your favourite school subjects.

10

1 Write the words.

Tom and Sue

____

Jane

____

Bob

____

Polly

____

Mark and Emma

____

2 Answer the questions.

What is Jane doing? She is doing the ____________________.

What about Bob? ____________________.

What are Mark and Emma doing? ____________________.

What about Tom and Sue? ____________________.

And Polly? ____________________.

3 Find the words. Circle and draw lines.

1 Look, read and write the names.

Lucy	Peter	Anne	John	Terry

Who is doing the washing-up? ____________

Who is doing the tidying? ____________

Who is doing the shopping? ____________

Who is doing the cleaning? ____________

Who is doing the gardening? ____________

2 Look and write.

 enjoys

 hates

 doesn't mind

Anne   Anne enjoys swimming.

Wendy   ____________________.

Terry   ____________________.

Jean   ____________________.

Kate   ____________________.

John   ____________________.

Max   ____________________.

3 What about you?

What do you enjoy doing? ____________________.

What do you hate doing? ____________________.

What don't you mind doing? ____________________.

Dictionary skills

1 **Match.**

bone box boy boat boot bow

  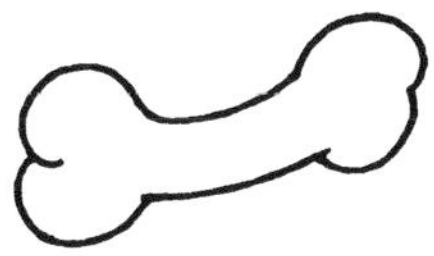   

2 **Write the words in ABC order.**

____

____

____

____

____

____

3 **Spelling.**
Look, listen and say.

one wolf

three wolves

one thief

two thieves

Write the words.

calf	knife	leaf	loaf	half

 $\frac{1}{2}$   

__________ __________ __________ __________ __________

Write the words.

   $\frac{1}{2}\ \frac{1}{2}\ \frac{1}{2}$ 

__________ __________ __________ __________ __________

Composition

1 **Look at the pictures.**

2 **Answer the questions and write the story.**
Use the words in brackets. (   )

Can Jim's mother do the housework? Why not? (because)
Is Jim a nice boy? Can he help his mother? (and)
Is his mother pleased?
What does Jim's mother give him?
What must he do?
Does Jim work hard? What has he done two hours later? (and)
Who is looking for Jim? Can she find him? (but)
What is Jim doing?
Is he tired? What is the matter with his back? (and)

Revision

1 **Write the past participles.**

break ______ eat ______ take ______

win ______ buy ______ make ______

Write. What have they just done?

A

B

C

D

E

F

A: ______.

B: ______.

C: ______.

D: ______.

E: ______.

F: ______.

2 **Write the past participles.**

live ______ have ______ play ______ know ______

Make sentences with *for* or *since*.

July ______.

20 years ______.

6 months ______.

1996 ______.

3 Make sentences.

Cars	grown	farmer
Bread	sewn	baker
Vegetables	sold	shoemaker
Shoes	made	greengrocer
Jackets	baked	mechanic
Wheat	mended	tailor

Cars are mended by the mechanic.

____.

____.

____.

____.

____.

4 Make questions.

Where _______________________________________?

Cotton is grown in hot countries.

How long ____________________________________?

They have been living here for two years.

How many ___________________________________?

Paul has written lots of poems.

What _______________________________________?

Alex has just won a prize.

Why ____?

We have been running because it is late.

5 Finish the sentences.

Use *enough*. Choose from these words:

long	fast	old	strong	sweet

I can't lift the suitcase because _______________________________.

I can't eat these grapes because _______________________________.

I can't wear this belt because _______________________________.

She can't go to school because _______________________________.

He can't win the race because _______________________________.

11

1 **Finish the sentences.**
Draw lines.

100 years ago schools were	very expensive.
Children did not learn to write	uniforms.
They used to write	with biros.
Books used to be	on slates.
Teachers used to be	very different.
Children did not wear	strict.

2 **Write the subjects.**

science	history	geography	sports	mathematics

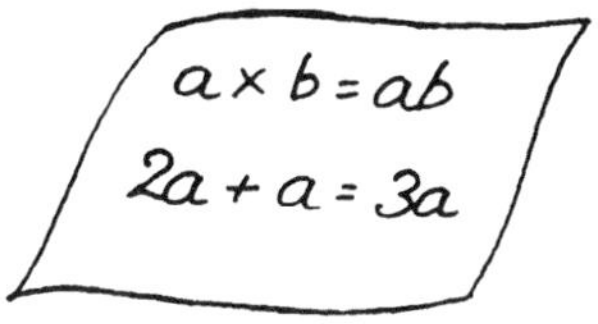

_______________ ✔

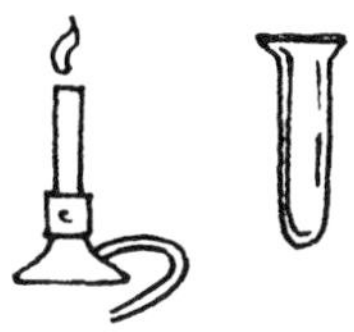

_______________ ✘

_______________ ✔

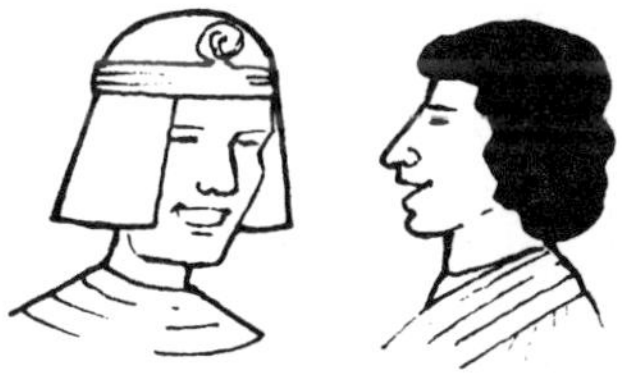

_______________ ✔

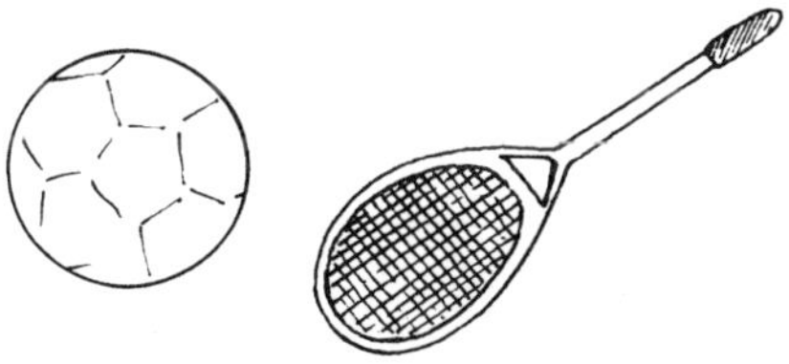

_______________ ✘

Children used to do _______________________________ .

They did not do _______________________________ .

_______________________________ .

_______________________________ .

_______________________________ .

1 Read and fill in the information.

When he was a young man, Ted used to live in Australia.
One of Ted's friends used to live in America and the other used to live in Egypt.
Bill used to be a pilot.
The man who lived in Egypt was a doctor.
One of the men was a good photographer.
The pilot used to play the violin very well.
The third man used to win prizes for swimming.
One of them used to be a farmer and he was no good at taking photos.

	Bill	Ted	Harry
country			
job			
hobbies			

2 Write about the three men.

When he was a young man, Bill used to ______________________________.

He ______________________ and ______________________.

When he was a young man, Ted ______________________________.

He ______________________ and ______________________.

When he was a young man, Harry ______________________________.

____.

1 Find the toys and games in the doll's house.

Look across → and down ↓.

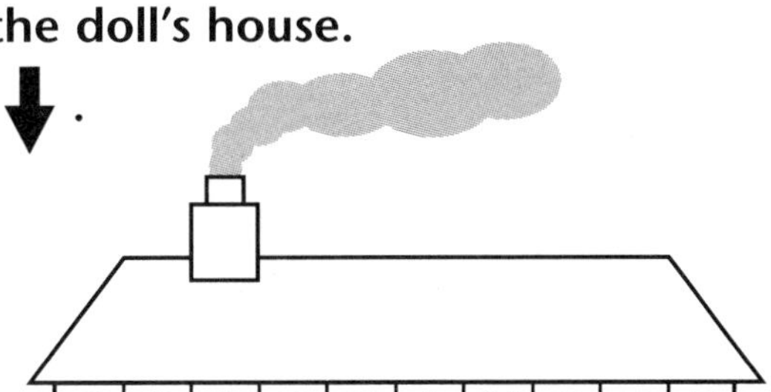

S	K	I	P	P	I	N	G	R	F
T	O	H	B	I	K	E	S	N	S
B	S	O	L	D	I	E	R	S	K
L	D	O	P	A	T	R	O	X	A
H	O	P	S	C	O	T	C	H	T
F	L	S	L	E	P	R	U	N	E
A	L	T	R	I	S	O	A	W	S
P	S	C	O	O	T	E	R	S	Y

2 Write the names.

bikes

____

____

____

____

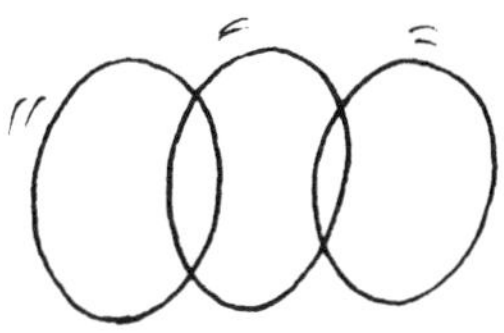
____

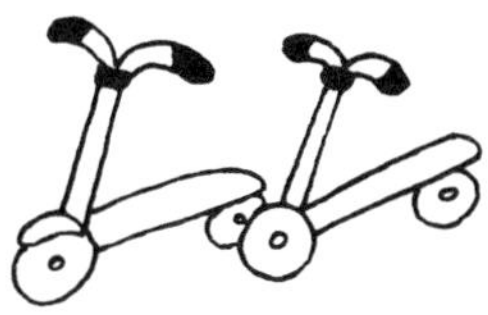
____

____

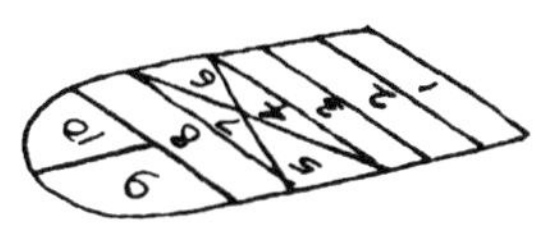
____

3 What do you do with them?

Use these verbs: skip rock push spin roll pull ride

You ride on it.

__________.

__________.

__________.

__________.

__________.

__________.

1 Who said what? Look and write.

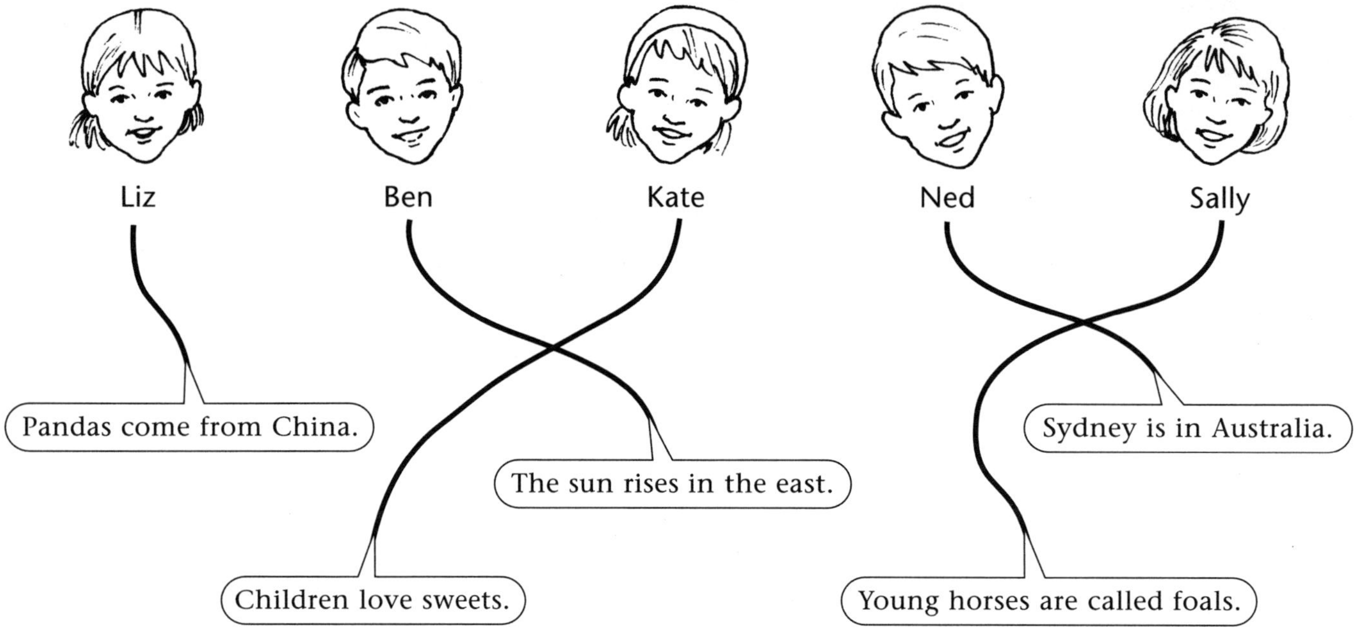

Liz said that ______________________________

Ben ______________________________

Kate ______________________________

Ned said ______________________________

Sally ______________________________

2 Ask and write notes.

Do you have any brothers and sisters? Tell me about them.
Do you have any pets? Tell me about them.
Do you have any hobbies? Tell me about them.

3 Write.

Like this: *John told me that he has two brothers and one sister.*

____

____

____

____

____

____

Dictionary skills

1 **More than one meaning.**
Look at this.

> **fast¹** (fɑːst) *adj* **-er, -est 1** quick. **2** (of a clock or watch) showing a time later than the real time. **3** not easily moved: *The mud has stuck fast to my shoes.* **4** (of colours) not fading. ● *adv* quickly.
> **fast²** *vi* eat no food, esp. for religious reasons. ● *nc* an act or time of fasting.

'fast' has 4 meanings:

adjective	(*adj*)	He has a <u>fast</u> car.
adverb	(*adv*)	He drives <u>fast</u>.
verb	(*v*)	He <u>is fasting</u>. (not eating)
noun	(*n*)	He is on a <u>fast</u>. (a time of not eating)

2 **Look.**

How many meanings can you find for these words?
Can you write sentences to show the meanings?

sweet

> **sweet** (swiːt) *adj* **-er, -est 1** having or being like the taste of sugar. **2** pleasant; nice: *a sweet smile; sweet music.* **3** fresh: *the sweet smell of clean sheets.* ● *nc Brit* **1** a small piece of boiled sugar, a piece of chocolate, etc. **2** *Brit* a sweet dish served as a part of a meal. **sweetheart** (ˈswiːthɑːt) *nc* a person who is loved by another of the opposite sex. **sweeten** (ˈswiːtən) *vti* make or become sweet or sweeter. **sweetly** *adv* **sweetness** *nu* being sweet.

____

____

shout

> **shout** (ʃaʊt) *nc* a loud cry. ● *vti* call or say loudly: *He shouted with joy; She shouted a warning.*

____

____

fine

> **fine¹** (faɪn) *adj* **-r, -st 1** (of weather) bright and clear; with the sun shining. **2** beautiful; good; pleasing: *fine clothes.* **3** of very small pieces; thin: *Salt is a fine white substance; fine cloth.* **fine arts** painting, drawing, and sculpture. **finely** *adv*
> **fine²** *nc* a sum of money to be paid as a punishment for breaking a law or a rule. ● *vt* demand a fine from (someone).

____

____

____

Composition

1 **Talk about the pictures and then write.**

Great-grandmother's childhood

Where did she live?
Who did she live with?
Did she have any pets?

Was her teacher strict?
What subject was she good at?
What subject was she bad at?

Did she play after school? What did she ride on?
What did she do with the doll's house?
Was she happy?

When great-grandmother was a little girl, ______________________________

____

____

____

She used to go to school. ______________________________

____

____

____

After school she used to ______________________________

____

____

____

12

1 **Look at this and answer the questions.**

What is this man? ____________________.

What is he trying to reach? ____________________.

What is he carrying? ____________________.

Are the rocks difficult to climb? ____________________.

What is the weather like? ____________________.

What is going to happen soon? ____________________.

2 **Cover the picture and write. What did he say?**

He said that he did not have a radio. — I ____________________

He said that his equipment was heavy. — ____________________

He said that the rocks were very steep. — ____________________

He said that he could reach the summit. — ____________________

He said that a blizzard was coming. — ____________________

Look back and check.

1 Underline the verbs in the speech bubbles. Then write the verbs.

It is cold.	He said that it _was_ cold.
We are at the summit.	He said that they ________ at the summit.
The mountain looks beautiful.	He said that the mountain ________ beautiful.
I can see the camp.	He said that he ________ see the camp.
We're coming down.	He said that they ____________ down.
I have heavy equipment.	He said that he ________ heavy equipment.

2 Write ***said*** or ***told***.

John ________ his teacher that he was ill.

Maggie ________ that she was feeling tired.

The boys ________ that they could play football.

Mum ________ Alex and Joe that dinner was ready.

Miss Walker ________ that she enjoyed travelling.

3 What did Jake say? What did he tell Marty?

I love climbing.

Marty, I can see the summit.

A blizzard is coming.

I have the radio, Marty.

____

____

____

____

1 Number the pictures in order.

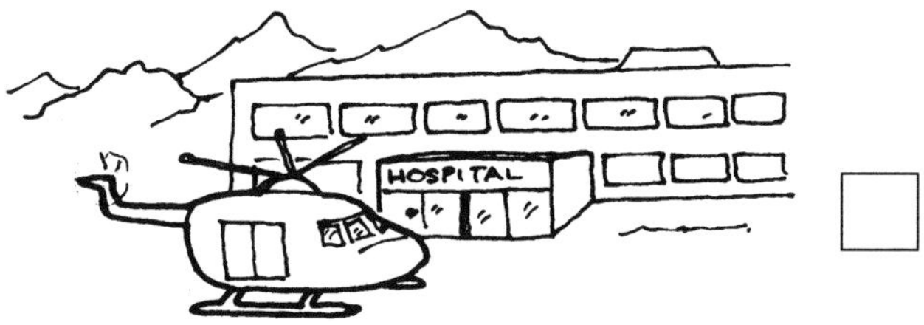

2 Write a sentence about each picture.

1 Last week ______________________________.

2 ______________________________.

3 ______________________________.

4 ______________________________.

5 ______________________________.

6 ______________________________.

7 ______________________________.

3 Find the opposites. Draw lines.

save enjoy

push  buy

take off difficult

inside spend

easy different

the same pull

sell hate

land outside

1 Find the opposites. Draw lines.

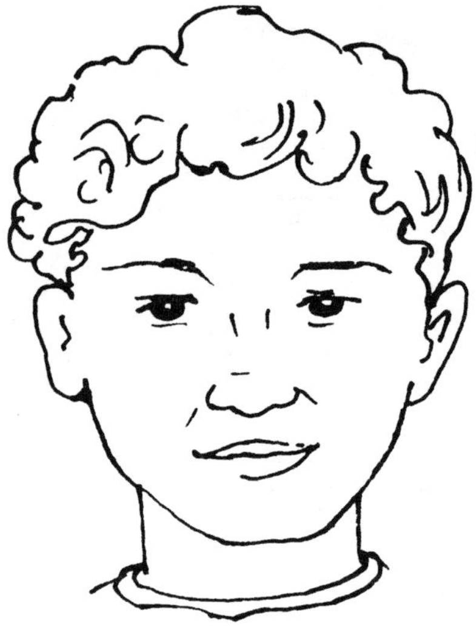

I'm happy.	Billy can't water-ski.
Sunny Island is great!	I'm not happy here.
I'm enjoying myself.	I don't like Sunny Island.
I can water-ski.	I'm not having a good time.

2 What did they say? Write like this.

Billy said he was happy but Mandy said she was not happy.

1 Billy said ______________________________.

2 ______________________________.

3 ______________________________.

3 Write in the speech bubbles.

Mandy said she wanted an ice cream. ______________________________

Billy said he was going to water-ski. ______________________________

Mandy told Billy he couldn't water-ski. ______________________________

Billy told Mandy he liked Sunny Island. ______________________________

Dictionary skills

1 **Verbs.**

You can find lists of verbs in the dictionary.
You can see the infinitive, the past tense and the past participle.

Infinitive	Past Tense	Past Participle
take	took	taken
teach	taught	taught
tear	tore	torn
tell	told	told
think	thought	thought
thrive	throve thrived	thriven, thrived
throw	threw	thrown
thrust	thrust	thrust
tread	trod	trodden, trod
unbend	unbent	unbent
undergo	underwent	undergone
understand	understood	understood
undertake	undertook	undertaken
underwrite	underwrote	underwritten
undo	undid	undone
upset	upset	upset
wake	woke, waked	waked, woken
wear	wore	worn
weave	wove	woven

2 **Look and write.**

Find the past tense of: tell ______________ think ______________

throw ______________ wake ______________

Find the past participle of: tear ______________ understand ______________

take ______________ weave ______________

3 **Complete these sentences.**

She has ______________ us for two years. (teach)

Yesterday I ______________ my books to school. (take)

Has John ______________ up yet? (wake)

She ______________ her dress last night. (tear)

He ______________ her the ball but she did not catch it. (throw)

Composition

1 **Talk about the pictures and then write the story.**

Last week Bill and Ben ______________________________

____

____

A woman ______________________________

____

____

The sea rescue team ______________________________

____

____

13

1 What are they? Draw lines.

calculator

vacuum cleaner

dishwasher

computer

sewing machine

washing machine

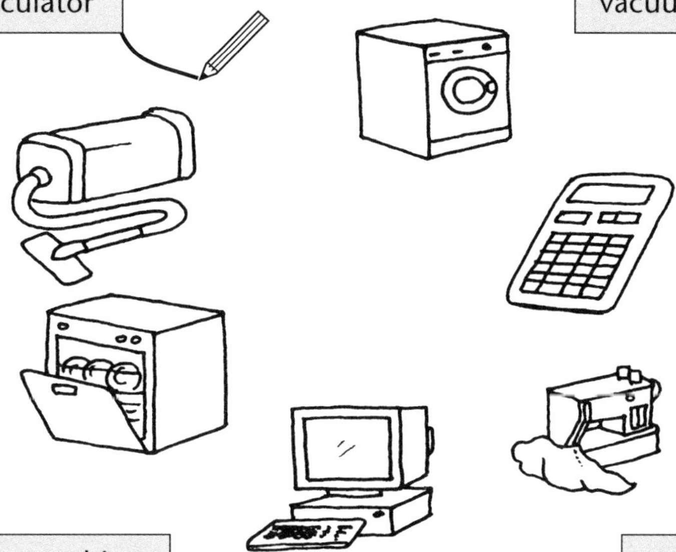

2 Read and write the words.

You do the washing-up with it. ____________________

You do mathematics with it. ____________________

It looks like a television. ____________________

Clothes are washed in it. ____________________

Clothes are sewn by it. ____________________

You clean carpets with it. ____________________

3 Complete the sentences with these words.

by an Englishman	on a cart	of wood	by a horse	in 1946	in America

The first washing machine was invented ____________________ .

It was made ____________________ .

The first computer was built ____________________ .

It was invented ____________________ .

The first vacuum cleaner was placed ____________________ .

It was pulled from house to house ____________________ .

1 Look and write.

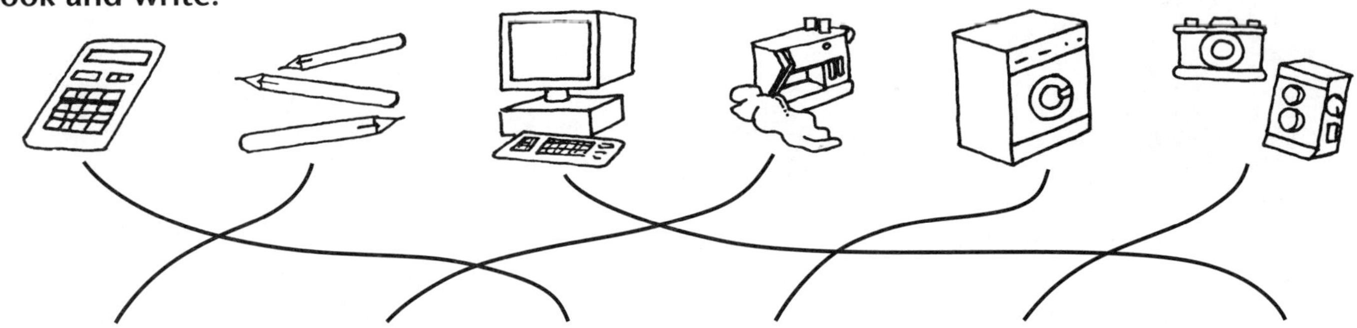

400 years ago | 1856 | 1642 | 1897 | 200 years ago | 1946

The calculator was invented in ______________________

____

____

____

____

____

2 Read, look and write ✔ or ✗.

Coins (metal money) were invented by the Greeks. ☐

The first scissors were made by the Chinese. ☐

A water clock was invented by the Greeks. ☐

A loom (a machine for weaving cloth) was invented by the Chinese. ☐

Fireworks were invented by the Greeks. ☐

The first umbrellas were made by the Egyptians. ☐

3 Write. Correct the false sentences. Use *not*.

The first scissors were not made by the Chinese.

______________________.

______________________.

______________________.

1 **What do you remember about the Kariba Dam?**
Write questions for these answers.

Use: What? Why? When? How? Where?

______________________________? It was built on the Zambezi river.

______________________________? They were given new homes.

______________________________? They were trapped because the water rose.

______________________________? They were rescued by boats.

______________________________? They were taken away from the lake.

2 **Describe the Kariba Dam.**

Include these words: wall road valley lake

____

____

____

____

____

____

1 Read about the Statue of Liberty.
Write the missing words.

island	built	inside	France	visited	woman	stairs
in her right hand		in the world	New York	given	crown	

If you go to ________________ , you will see the Statue of Liberty. It stands on an ____________ in the sea. It was _____________ to America by the people of France and it was ____________ in 1876.

It is a statue of a woman. She is wearing a ________________ and she is carrying a torch ____________________________ . It is one of the largest statues ___________________ . It is ______________ by thousands of tourists every year. You can go into the statue. You can walk up the ______________ and stand ________________ its head.

2 Who did it? What did it?

Write the past participles: grow _______________ build _______________

make _______________ take _______________ bake _______________

Write.

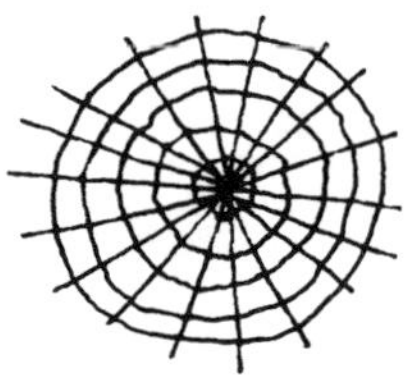

It was made by a spider.

____ .

____ .

____ .

____ .

Dictionary skills

1 **Match.**

stripes string stream

shell sheep shed

  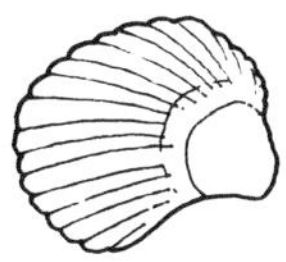

monkey money monster

2 **Write in ABC order.**

3 **Spelling.**
What is the difference?

one toy	two toys
one day	two days

one lady	two ladies
one city	two cities

Write the words.

baby	babies	holiday	________	boy	________
hobby	________	family	________	monkey	________
canary	________	key	________	factory	________

Composition

1 Which places in your town are visited by tourists?
Make a list.

2 Choose two places. Draw them and write about them.
Where are they? When were they built? What is interesting about them?

14

1 **Finish the sentences.**

If Sally had a horse,	he would buy a new camera.
If Joe had some skates,	she would do the gardening.
If Alex had more money,	she would ride it every day.
If Mrs Gordon had more time,	he would drive to the beach.
If Mr Gordon had a new car,	he would jump and spin.

2 **Write the names.**

computer	mountain bike	walkman	in-line skates	watch	electric guitar

______________________ ☐

______________________ ☐

______________________ ☐

______________________ ☐

______________________ ☐

______________________ ☐

Which things would you like? Write ✔.

3 **Write about the things you would like.**

If I had a ____________________ , I would ______________________________________

____

____

____

1 Write.
What would they buy if they had enough money?

Joe

Sue and Fred

Sally

Mark

Ann and Bill

Alex

If Joe had enough money, he would ______________________________.

If Sally ______________________________.

If Sue and Fred ______________________________.

Mark would ____________________ if ____________________.

Ann and Bill ______________________________.

Alex ______________________________.

2 What about you?

What would you buy if you had 1 pound?

50 pounds?

500 pounds?

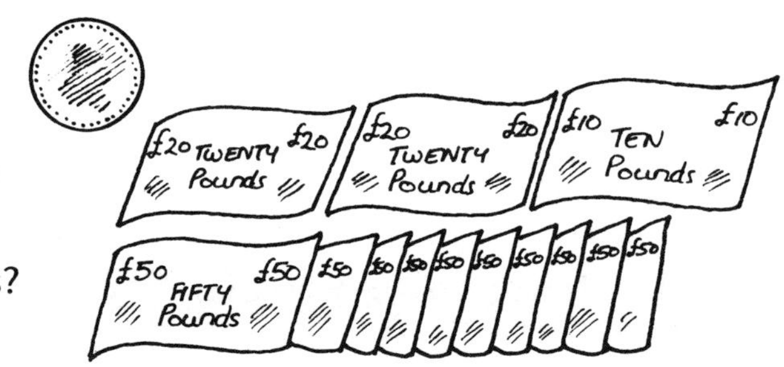

______________________________.

______________________________.

______________________________.

1 What are the words?

2 Write about it.

If you were on a desert island,

what would you do? ______________________________.

what would you eat? ______________________________.

what would you like? ______________________________.

what would you dislike? ______________________________.

how would you feel? ______________________________.

who (or what) would you miss? ______________________________.

1 Can you name these things?

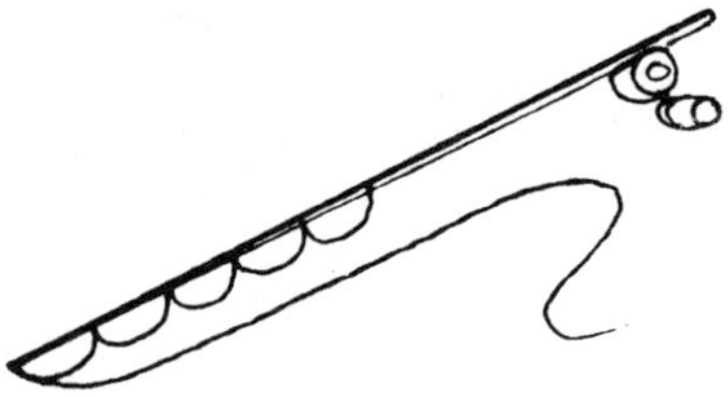

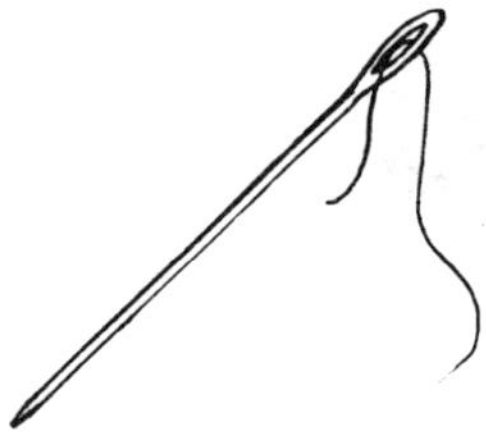

______________________ ______________________ ______________________

______________________ ______________________ ______________________

2 Write sentences.

Use these words:

sailor	fisherman	photographer
mountaineer	teacher	tailor

If I was a sailor, I would need a yacht.

If I had a yacht, I would sail round the world.

If I was a ______________, I would ______________________________.

If I had a ______________, I would ______________________________.

____.

____.

____.

____.

____.

____.

____.

____.

Dictionary skills

1 **Adjectives.**

In the dictionary you can find the comparative and superlative of adjectives.

fine

> **fine**[1] (faɪn) *adj* **-r, -st** **1** (of weather) bright and clear; with the sun shining. **2** beautiful; good; pleasing: *fine clothes.* **3** of very small

great

> **great**[1] (greɪt) *adj* **-er, -est** **1** large in size or number. **2** lasting a long time; unusually long: *a great while; He lived to a great age.*

big

> **big** (bɪg) *adj* **-ger, -gest** **1** large. **2** on a grand scale: *He has big ideas.* **3** generous in spirit:

bad

> **bad** (bæd) *adj* **worse, worst** **1** of poor quality. **2** morally wrong; evil. **3** harmful. **4** unsuitable for a particular purpose. **5** serious:

2 **Complete these sentences.**

His car is ________________ than hers. (big)

This is the ________________ place in the world. (fine)

It was the ________________ film I have ever seen. (bad)

That's the ________________ book I have ever read. (great)

Your work is ________________ than your sister's. (bad)

3 **Spelling.**

Look at these adjectives and adverbs.
What is the difference?

quiet	quietly
slow	slowly

noisy	noisily
happy	happily

Write the adverbs.

The children are playing ________________ . (noisy)

She smiled ________________ . (pretty)

He runs very ________________ . (quick)

They ate their lunch ________________ . (hungry)

She plays the trumpet ________________ . (loud)

The man shouted ________________ . (angry)

Composition

1 **Read this poem.**

If I could be an animal, I'd be a tiger.
  I'd walk through the jungle and roar in the night.
If I could be a bird, I'd be an eagle.
  I'd fly high in the mountains and nest in the clouds.
If I could travel anywhere, I'd go to the North Pole.
  I'd build an igloo and look for polar bears.
If I could be anyone, I'd be a funny clown.
  I'd run around the circus ring and make the children laugh.
Well, I'm not a tiger and I'm not an eagle.
I'm not at the North Pole and I'm not a funny clown.

2 **Now you write a poem in the same way.**

If...

If I could be an animal, ______________________________

____

If I could be a bird, ______________________________

____

If I could travel anywhere, ______________________________

____

If I could be anyone, ______________________________

____

Well, I'm not ______________________________

I'm not ______________________________

But ______________________________

15

1 Look at the pictures.

1

2

3

4

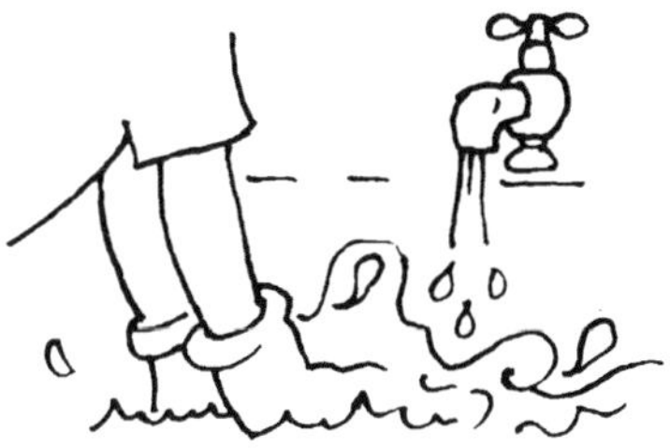

5

6

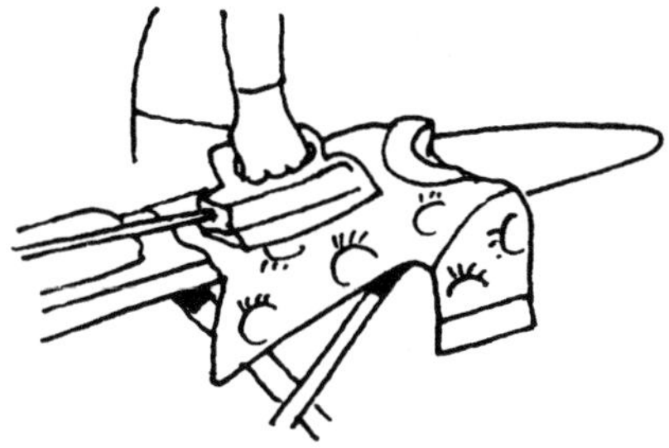

Read and write the numbers.

☐ Put the T-shirt in the bowl of dye and stir it.

☐ Hang the T-shirt up to dry.

☐ Make a pattern with the stones on the shirt.

☐ Take out the stones and iron the shirt.

☐ Rinse the T-shirt in cold water.

☐ Tie the stones into the T-shirt with string.

2 Look and write the instructions.

After you rinse the shirt, hang it up to dry.

Before you iron the shirt, ______________________________ .

Before you dye the shirt, ______________________________ .

After you dye the shirt, ______________________________ .

After you dry the shirt, ______________________________ .

1 Look at this.

Tom's morning:
get up - wash face - brush teeth - have breakfast - go to school

Tom's evening:
come home - play piano - do homework - have supper - go to bed

What will Tom do tomorrow?
Write the verbs.

After Tom gets up, he will wash his face.

After he ______ his face, he ______ his teeth.

Before he ______ to school, he ______ breakfast.

When he ______ home, he ______ piano.

He ______ his homework after he ______ piano.

He ______ supper before he ______ to bed.

2 Look at the pictures and write sentences.
What will they do?

She ______ before ______

After he ______, he ______

Before she ______, she ______

He ______ after ______

Dictionary skills

1 **Plurals.**

You can find the plurals of words in a dictionary.

baby

baby (ˈbeɪbɪ) *nc, pl* **-bies** 1 a young human. 2 *infml* a favourite project. 3 *infml* the youngest member of a group. ● *adj* of smaller size than usual. **babysit** (ˈbeɪbɪˌsɪt) *vi* stay in the house with small children while their parents are out. **babysitter** *nc*

knife

knife (naɪf) *nc, pl* **-ves** (vz) a metal blade with a sharp edge and a handle, used chiefly for cutting or as a weapon. ● *vt* stick a knife into (someone).

Write the plurals of these words:

lady	______	potato	______	calf	______
goose	______	sheep	______	child	______
piano	______	deer	______	tooth	______

lady (ˈleɪdɪ) *nc, pl* **-dies** 1 *polite* a woman. 2 a woman with a high position in society. **ladies** *infml. Brit nc, pl* **ladies** *(often with singular verb)* a public toilet for women. **Lady**

potato (pəˈteɪtəʊ) *nc, pl* **-es** a root that is nearly white inside, has brown or red skin, and is cooked and eaten as a vegetable: see picture at **vegetables. potato crisp** *US* **potato chip** See **crisp.**

calf[1] (kɑːf) *nc, pl* **calves** 1 (of cattle) a young cow or bull. 2 a young seal, elephant, etc. **calf**[2] *nc, pl* **calves** the back of the lower leg.

goose (guːs) *nc, pl* **geese** a bird that can swim and is larger than a duck.

sheep (ʃiːp) *nc, pl* **sheep** an animal kept for its wool and its meat. **sheepish** (ˈʃiːpɪʃ) *adj* 1 feeling foolish because of doing something wrong, stupid, etc. 2 not wanting to do something for fear of drawing attention

child (tʃaɪld) *nc, pl* **children** (ˈtʃɪldrən) 1 a young person up to the age of about fifteen. 2 a son or daughter. **childhood** *nc* 1 the condition of being a child. 2 the period when one is a child. **childless** *adj* not hav-

piano (pɪˈænəʊ) *nc, pl* **-s** a musical instrument with strings hit by pressing the keys: see picture at **musical instruments. pianist** (ˈpɪənɪst) *nc*

deer (dɪə*) *nc, pl* **deer** a graceful animal, the male having horns like the branches of a tree: see picture at **animals.**

tooth (tuːθ) *nc, pl* **teeth** 1 one of the set of bone-like parts of the mouth used chiefly for biting and chewing. 2 a tooth-like object on a comb, gear, etc. **toothache** (ˈtuːθeɪk) *nc* a pain in or near a tooth.

Composition

1 **Think about a market.**

Think about the stalls and the shops which you can see there. Choose 3 or 4 stalls (or shops). What can you buy at each one? Make notes.

2 **Describe a trip to the market.**

When did you go there? Who did you go with? What did you see? What did you buy?

At the market

Revision

1 **Read and look.**

Mr MacDonald comes from Scotland. Here are some of the things he used to do when he was young.

Write about Mr MacDonald. Use these verbs:

climb	wear	ride

He used to ______________________________

____

____

What did Mr MacDonald say? What did he tell Sally and Joe?

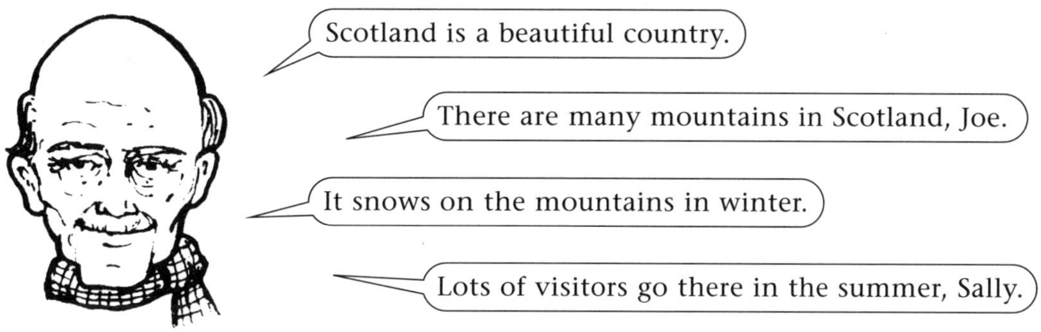

He said ______________________________.

He told Joe ______________________________.

He said ______________________________.

He told Sally ______________________________.

2 **Write the past participles.**

build __________ invent __________ wear __________ write __________

Make sentences.

Coins - invent - Greeks Coins were invented by the Greeks.

Kimonos - wear - men and women ______________________________.

A dam - build - beavers ______________________________.

A good story - write - reporter ______________________________.

3 What did the potter say?

The potter said that ____ .

He said that ____ .

____ .

____ .

4 Write 'said' or 'told'.

The potter ___________ that he loved his job.

He ___________ the girls that the kiln was a very hot oven.

He ___________ them that he painted his pots.

He ___________ they were not expensive.

5 Complete the sentences.

If I ________________ a potter, I ________________ big pots. (be, make)

I ________________ necklaces if I ________________ a jeweller. (make, be)

If I ________________ some wood, I ________________ a mask. (have, carve)

I ________________ my baskets if I ________________ a basket maker. (sell, be)

16

1 **What is wrong? Underline the mistakes.**

The Great Pyramid was built on the east bank of the Nile.

A few workmen helped to build it.

Stone was brought from Aswan by camel.

After twenty years the pyramid was started.

The pharaoh was buried next to the pyramid.

Correct the sentences.

____

____

____

____

____

2 **Finish the sentences.**

The pharaoh told the architects 	to build the pyramid.
He told the engineers	to bury him in the pyramid.
He told his people	to draw the plans.

3 **Write in the speech bubbles.**

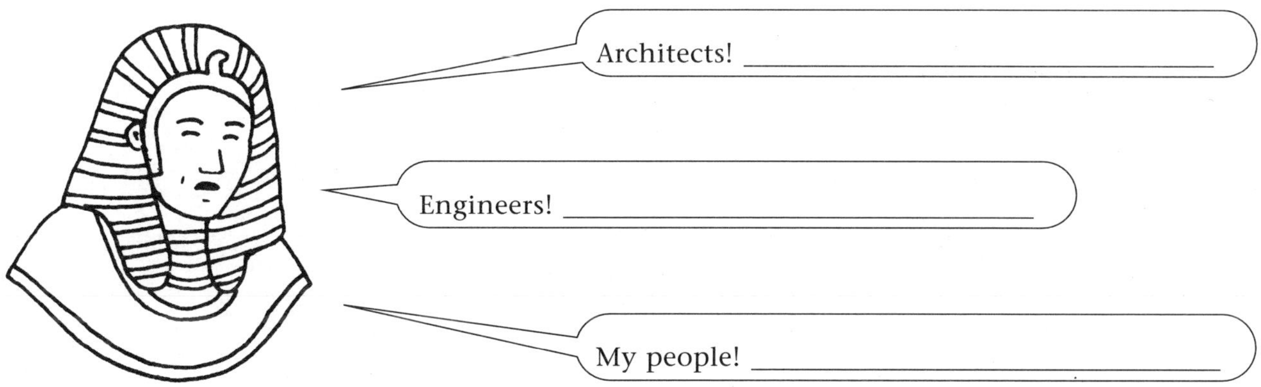

1 What did the pharaoh tell his people?
Write his commands.

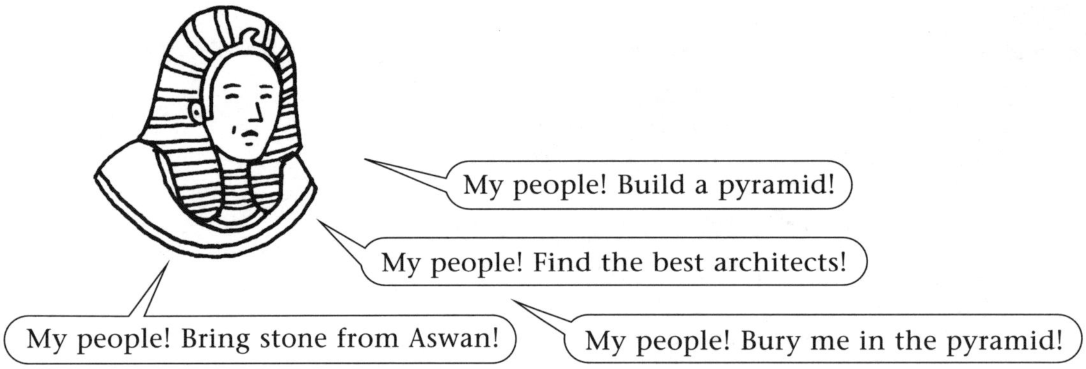

He told his people to build a pyramid.

He told them ______________________________ .

______________________________ .

______________________________ .

2 Look at this.

The teacher told the children to sit down.

The teacher asked the children to sit down.

Write the commands.
Use *told* or *asked*.

John! Be quiet!

Bob! Stop talking!

Jenny, please work harder.

Meg, do your work, please.

Mark, do your homework.

Children, please open your books.

______________________________ .

______________________________ .

______________________________ .

______________________________ .

______________________________ .

______________________________ .

1 **What is the word?**

The first kings of Egypt were buried in __ __ __ ☐ __ __ __ __ .

Howard Carter was looking for Tutankhamun's __ ☐ __ __ .

A boy was carrying water in a __ ☐ __ .

It was hot and the workmen were __ ☐ __ __ __ __ __ .

The boy kicked the earth with his ☐ __ __ __ .

__ __ __ ☐ __ went down to a door.

There were four ☐ __ __ __ __ in the tomb.

Put the letters in the squares in a different order.
They make a word. What is it?

☐ ☐ ☐ ☐ ☐ ☐ ☐

2 **Look at these words.**

necklace	kite	sofa	jacket	trumpet	
top	bracelet	stool	violin	dress	chair
ring	shirt	rocking horse	piano		

Sort the words into 5 groups.
Give each group a title.
Add two more things to each group.

______	______	______	______	______

1 What did Jenny's mum say?

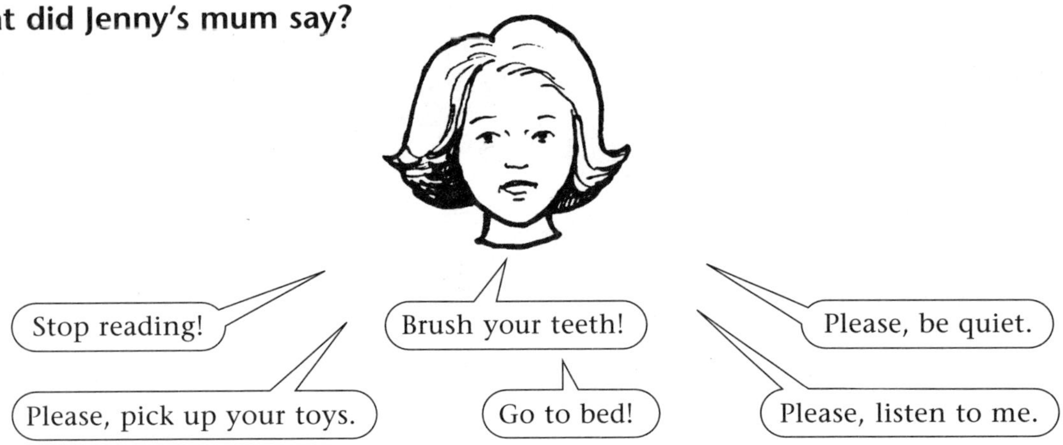

Write.

She told Jenny ______________________________.

______________________________.

______________________________.

She asked Jenny ______________________________.

______________________________.

______________________________.

2 Ask Jenny.
Write in the speech bubbles.

Please, Jenny, ______________________.

______________________.

______________________.

______________________.

______________________.

Dictionary skills

1 **Match.**

pyramid
camera
mask
plane
broom
loaf
necklace
calf
branch
prize

2 **Put the words in ABC order.**

____
____
____
____
____
____
____
____
____
____

3 **Spelling.**
Add the missing letters.

l ___ ___ f

g ___ ___ t

p ___ ___ nt

m ___ ___ se

___ ___ ght

c ___ ___ n

br ___ ___ m

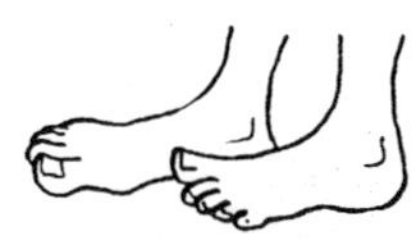
f ___ ___ t

r ___ p ___

c ___ g ___

sm ___ l ___

t ___ n ___

Composition

1 **Look and talk about the story.**

Where did Wendy and Peter go?
What were they carrying?

What did Wendy say? What did Peter say?
What did Peter ask Wendy?

What did the children start to do?
What did Wendy say?

What did the children pull out of the hole?

Was Wendy excited?
What did she tell Peter to do?

What was inside the box?
Were the children surprised?

2 **Write the story.**

17

1 Choose the right answer.

The Wright brothers were American. ☐
English. ☐

The Montgolfier brothers were English. ☐
French. ☐

Alcock and Brown flew across the Atlantic. ☐
flew a hot air balloon. ☐

The Wright brothers' plane could fly because it had an engine. ☐
it had passengers. ☐

Before the Wright brothers' flight, people had flown in hot air balloons. ☐
Concorde had crossed the Atlantic. ☐

After the Wright brothers had flown their plane, the Montgolfier brothers built a hot air balloon. ☐
Alcock and Brown flew across the Atlantic. ☐

2 Number the pictures in order.

☐

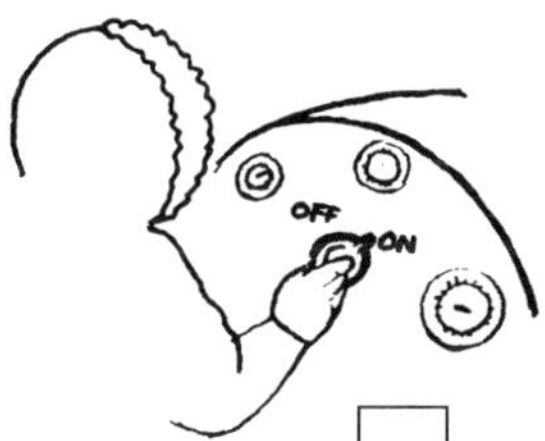

☐

☐

☐

☐

Finish the sentences.

After the pilot had climbed into the plane, he ______________________________ .

After he had started the engine, the plane ______________________________ .

After the plane had flown, it ______________________________ .

1 Look at this.

Mrs Brown went shopping. Where did she go and what did she buy?

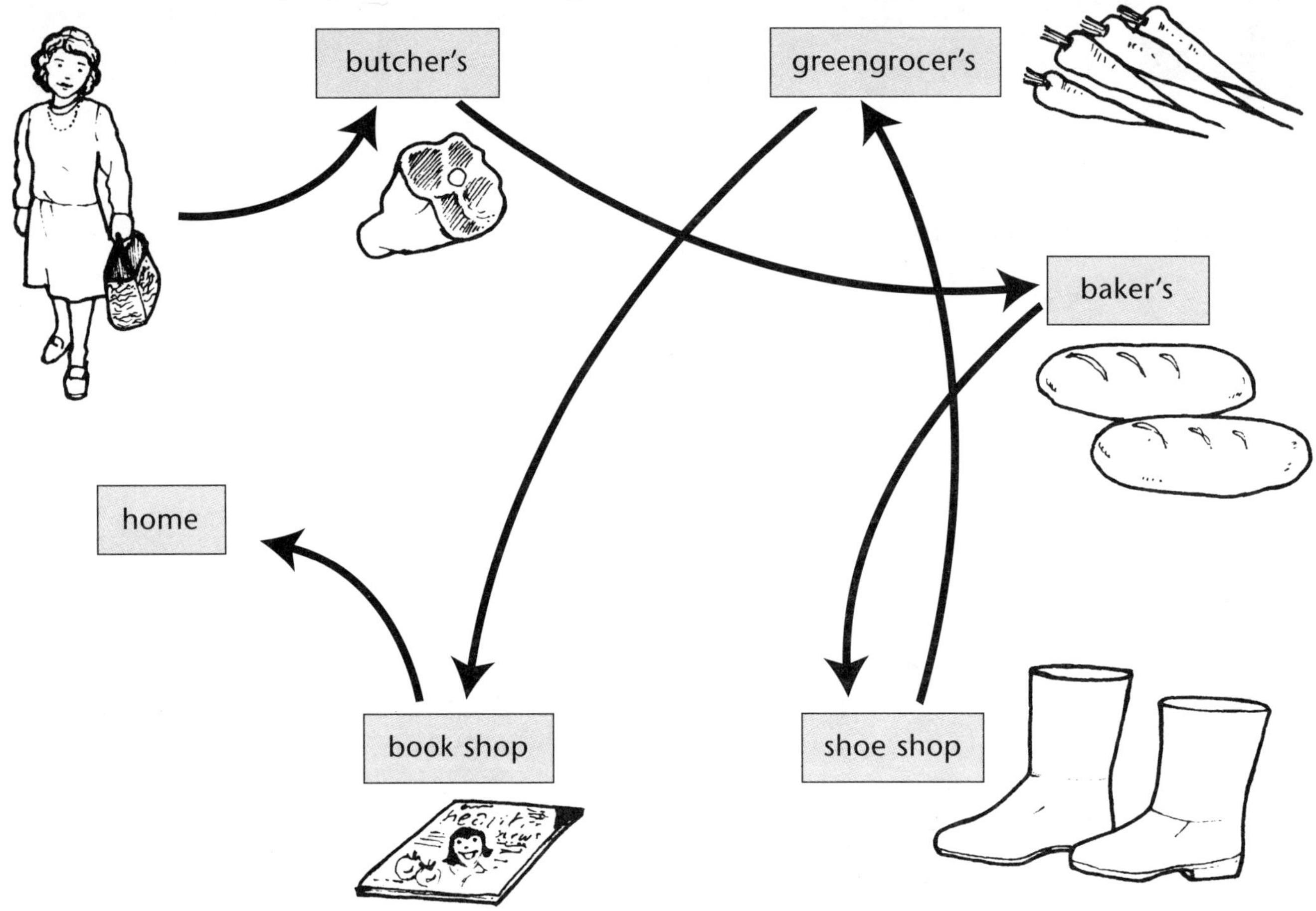

2 Make sentences.

baker's	She went to the baker's but before that she had gone to the butcher's.
book shop	______________________________.
shoe shop	______________________________.
home	______________________________.

After she had bought some carrots, she bought a magazine.

______________________________.

______________________________.

______________________________.

1 **Write the words.**

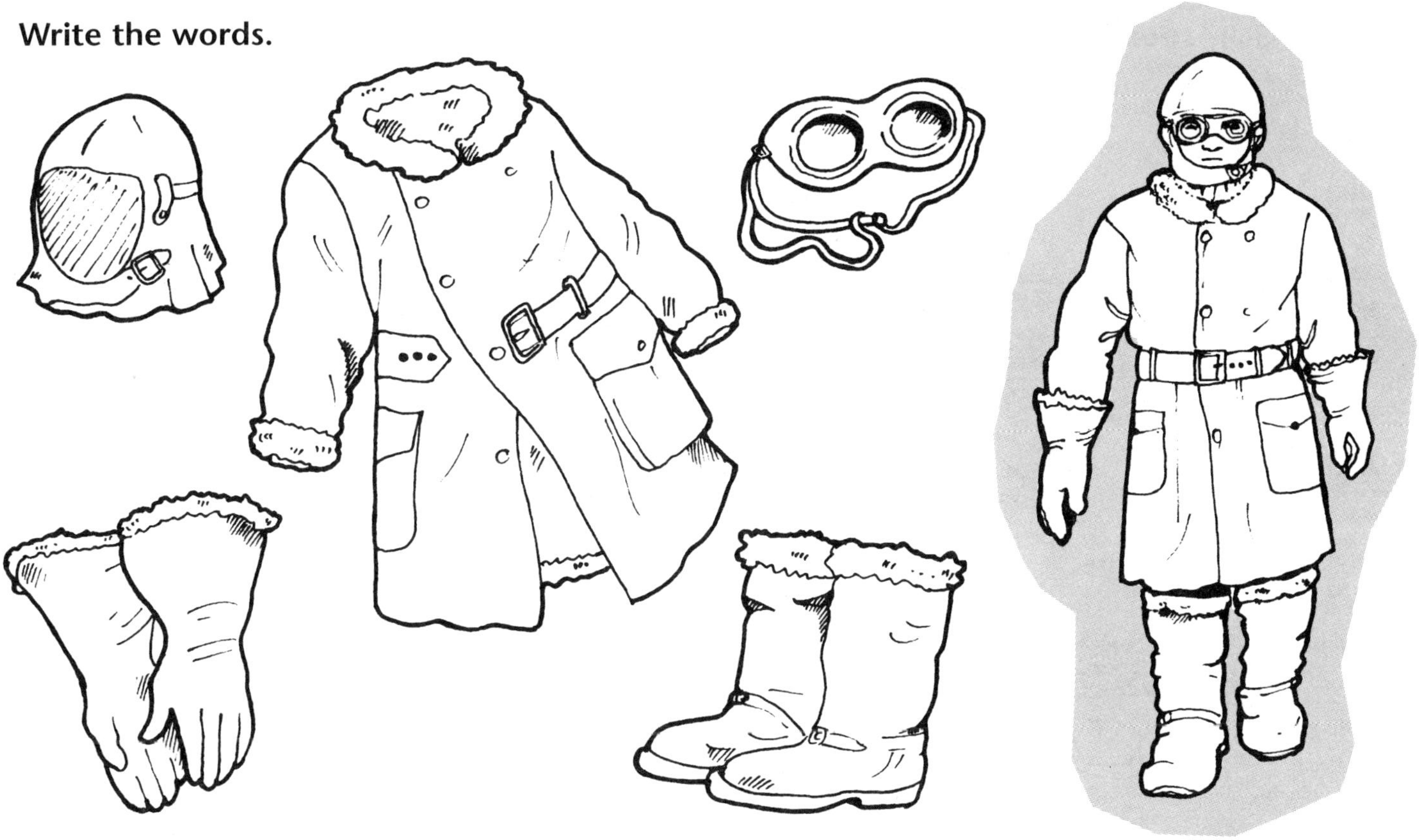

e o g g l s g	l b t e	e o l s v g	f c u f s
________	________	________	________

a o l r l c	a t o c	t s o o b	m l e e t h
________	________	________	________

2 **Flying the first planes was very cold. How did a pilot keep warm? Finish the sentences.**

A leather coat with wool inside kept his body warm.

The woollen collar ______________________________ .

Long gloves ______________________________ .

Long boots ______________________________ .

Cuffs with buttons ______________________________ .

A leather helmet like a mask ______________________________ .

1 Look! Sally spoke to these people.

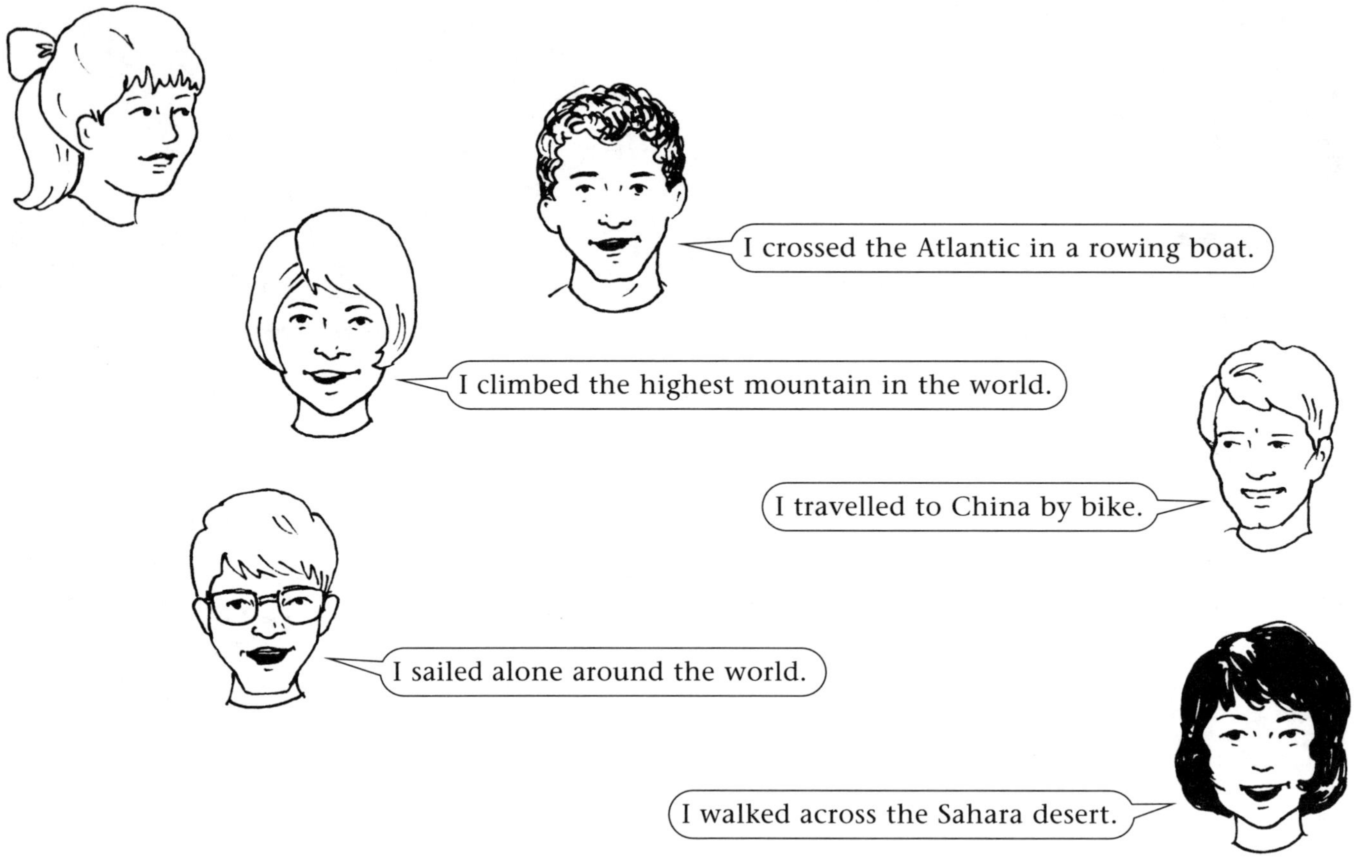

Write.

Sally met a man who had ______________________________ .

______________________________ .

______________________________ .

______________________________ .

______________________________ .

2 Read.

Sally spoke to a man who had rowed a small boat across the Atlantic. He left America in April. When he arrived home, he had been at sea for two months. He said it had been a dangerous journey because the weather had been bad. He was very happy to be home again because he had not seen his family for a long time.

3 Make questions. Use:

Who?	How?	What … like?	How long?

______________________________ ? He had travelled by boat.

______________________________ ? He had been at sea for two months.

______________________________ ? The weather had been very bad.

______________________________ ? He had not seen his family for ages.

Dictionary skills

1

English and American spellings and words.

Americans spell some words differently from English people. Your dictionary shows you this.

Look.

colour *US* **color** ('kʌlə*) *nc* **1** a quality of the light produced or reflected by something, such as red, green, or blue. **2** a paint with a particular colour. **3** the colour of a person's skin: *Colour makes no difference.* ● *vt* **1**

favour *US* **favor** ('feɪvə*) **1** *nu* being friendly, or kindly to; approval. **2** *nc* a

theatre *US* **theater** ('θɪətə*) *nc* **1** a building where plays, operas, etc., can be seen by the public. **2** a large room with each row of seats placed behind and higher than the one before, used for lectures, etc. **3** a place where important events happen. **theatrical**

centre *US* **center** ('sentə*) *nc* **1** a middle, esp. the point in the middle of a circle. **2** a place for a particular activity or purpose or where something is sold: *shopping centre; leisure centre.* **3** a group of politicians who are not far to the left or right. ● *vt* move (something) to a centre. **centre on, around,** or **round** have as a centre or cen-

Write E or US.

color ______ colourful ______ favourite ______ theater ______ centre ______

2

Americans use different words for some things.

Look.

pave (peɪv) *vt* cover (a road, floor, etc.) with flat stones or a material that sets hard. **pavement** *US* **sidewalk** *nc* a paved path for people walking next to a road.

petrol ('petrəl) *US* **gasoline** *ncu* a (type of) light, explosive oil made from petroleum and used to power car engines, etc. **petrol station** a place where petrol is sold.

waist (weɪst) *nc* **1** (the part of a garment covering) the part of the body between the ribs and the hip-bones. **2** the (narrower) middle part of an object. **waistcoat** ('weɪstkəʊt) *US, Australian* **vest** *nc* a buttoned, sleeveless, man's upper garment worn esp. under a jacket. **waistline** ('weɪstlaɪn) *nc* **1**

trousers ('traʊzəz) *n pl* also **pair of trousers** *chiefly US* **pants** a garment reaching from the waist down to any point on the legs, which it covers separately: see picture.

Write E or US.

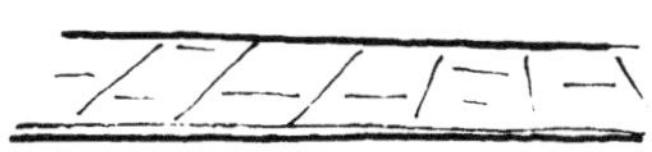

pavement ______

sidewalk ______

vest ______

waistcoat ______

pants ______

trousers ______

petrol ______

gasoline ______

Composition

1 **Write a letter to a friend.**
Describe a trip in a hot air balloon.
Remember to write your address and the date. (See WB5 Unit 9)

Write your letter in three parts. These questions can help you.

When did you make the trip? Who went with you? Why did you make the trip?

Where did you sit (or stand)? Where did you take off from? How long was the flight? Where did you land?

How did you feel? What could you see from the basket? Did you enjoy yourself?
Would you like to do it again?

18

1 Write the verbs.

Joe and Alex want to buy a present for Sally because it ____________ (be) her birthday soon. They ____________ (look) for a book now but they ____________ (not know) what to choose. Sally ____________ already ____________ (read) 'Clumsy Kevin' so Alex and Joe ____________ (not buy) this one. Sally ____________ (not like) scary stories so they ____________ (not choose) 'When the Moon is Full'. 'Call Detective Ross' ____________ (look) interesting. Sally ____________ (like) detective stories and she ____________ (not read) this one yet. They think that they ____________ (get) this book for her birthday.

2 Look at the books and write the words. Then answer the questions.

funny	interesting	frightening	sad

____________ ____________ ____________ ____________

Which book would you like to read? ________________________ .

Why? ________________________ .

Ask your friend.

Which book would he (she) like to read? ________________________ .

Why? ________________________ .

1 Circle the right word.

heavy or light?

sweet or sour?

cheap or expensive?

strong or weak?

well or ill?

interesting or boring?

Write sentences.

The suitcase was so heavy that ______________________.

______________________.

______________________.

______________________.

______________________.

______________________.

2 Write more sentences with *so* ... *that*.

Use these words:

clever	clumsy	frightened

______________________.

______________________.

______________________.

1 **Write the verbs.**

Choose from:

look	put	worry	catch	wear	ask
take off	go	say	take	help	find

Miss Jackson went to her room. She __________ the ring which she __________ and __________ it on the table. When she __________ again, the ring __________ . Someone __________ it! She __________ her nephew, Charles, to find the ring. '__________ , Aunt Emily!' he said. 'I __________ soon __________ the ring and I __________ the thief, too!'

2 **Read and write the words.**

uncle	aunt	cousin	nephew	niece	grandmother	great-grandfather

Your father's sister is your __________ .

Your brother's daughter is your __________ .

Your sister's son is your __________ .

Your mother's brother is your __________ .

Your father's sister's son is your __________ .

Your father's mother's father is your __________ .

1 Read.

'Alice in Wonderland' was written by an English writer called Lewis Carroll. The book was written more than 100 years ago but it is still popular with children today. Here is a part of the story:

1 Alice found herself in a dark room. There was a glass table in the corner and on the table there was a tiny gold key. Alice saw a very small door. She opened the door with the key. Outside there was a beautiful sunny garden. Alice wanted to go there but she was too big to go through the door.

2 Alice went back to the table. On the table there was a bottle with a label on it which said 'Drink me!'. Alice drank from the bottle and grew smaller and smaller. Now Alice could go through the door but it was shut again. Where was the key? It was on the table and now Alice could not reach it.

3 There was a glass box under the table. Inside the box there was a little cake with a label which said 'Eat me!' Alice ate the cake and grew taller and taller. 'Goodbye, feet!' she said. Her head was on the ceiling. Alice picked up the key but now she was too big to go through the little door.

4 She was very sad and she started to cry. Her tears made a pool of water and she had to start swimming.

2 Match these pictures to the four parts of the story. Write the numbers.

A ☐

B ☐

C ☐

D ☐

3 Write one sentence about each picture. Use *so* ... *that* ...

A ______________________________.

B ______________________________.

C ______________________________.

D ______________________________.

Dictionary skills

1 **Continents and countries.**

In your dictionary you can find the names of countries, the adjectives for those countries and the nouns for the people from those countries.

Look.

Canada (ˈkænədə)	Canadian (kəˈneɪdɪən)
Chad (tʃæd)	Chadian (-dɪən)
Chile (ˈtʃɪlɪ)	Chilean (-lɪən)
China (ˈtʃaɪnə)	Chinese (ˌtʃaɪniːz)
Denmark (ˈdenmɑːk)	Danish (ˈdeɪnɪʃ), Dane (deɪn)
Dominican Republic (dəˈmɪnɪkən rɪˈpʌblɪk)	Dominican (-kən)
Ecuador (ˈekwədɔː*)	Ecuadorian (ˌekwəˈdɔːrɪən)
Egypt (ˈɪːdʒɪpt)	Egyptian (ɪˈdʒɪpʃən)
Europe (ˈjʊərəp)	European (ˌjʊərəˈpɪən)
Fiji (ˌfiːˈdʒiː)	Fijian (ˌfɪːˈdʒiːən)
Finland (ˈfɪnlənd)	Finnish (ˈfɪnɪʃ), Finn (fɪn)
France (frɑːns)	French (frentʃ), Frenchman (ˈfrentʃmən)
Italy (ˈɪtəlɪ)	Italian (ɪˈtælɪən)
Jamaica (dʒəˈmeɪkə)	Jamaican (-kən)
Japan (dʒəˈpæn)	Japanese (ˌdʒæpəˈniːz)
Java (ˈdʒɑːvə)	Javanese (ˌdʒɑːvəˈniːz)
Jordan (ˈdʒɔːdən)	Jordanian (dʒɔːˈdeɪnɪən)

Write the words.

a city in Europe: a ________________ city

a song from Japan: a ________________ song.

a stamp from Italy: an ________________ stamp

a lake in Canada: a ________________ lake

a person from Finland : a ________________

a man from France: a ________________

a person from Egypt: an ________________

a person from China: a ________________

A Dane comes from ________________

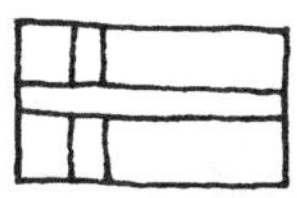

French cheese comes from ________________

A Jordanian necklace comes from ________________

A European river is in ________________

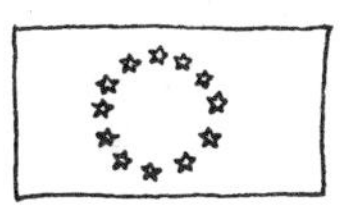

Composition

1 **Do you have a favourite book?**
Write about it.

Write your composition in four parts.
These questions will help you.

1) What is your favourite book called?
   When did you read it? How did you find the book?
   (a present? from the library?)
2) What is the book about? What is the story?
3) Who are the people in the book?
4) Why do you like the book?

My favourite book

Draw a cover for your book.

19

1 <u>Underline</u> **the mistakes.**

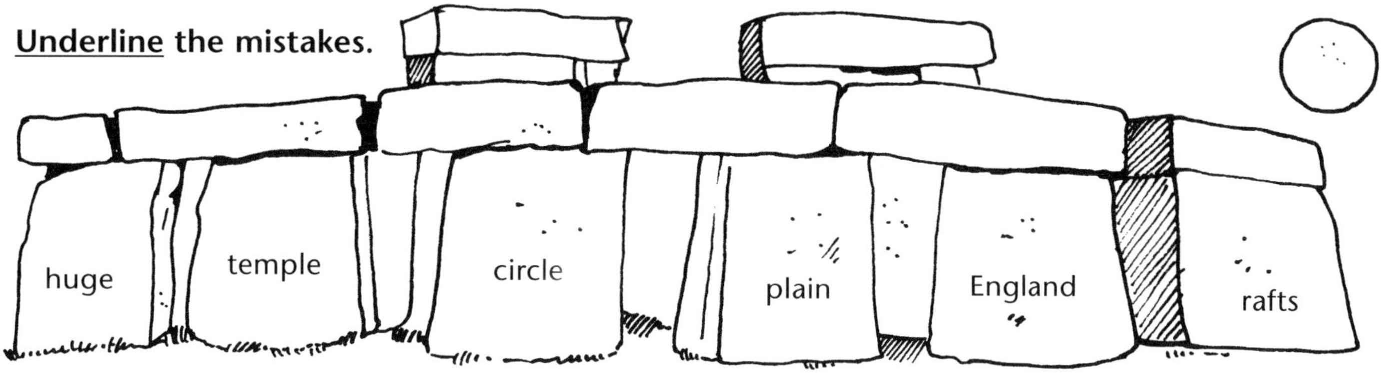

Stonehenge is in America.

Some stones were brought on carts.

The stones are tiny.

Stonehenge was built on a mountain.

The stones were placed in a square.

Stonehenge was used as a tomb.

Correct the sentences.

The words on Stonehenge can help you.

2 **Make sentences.**

Stonehenge - stand - plain - thousands

Stonehenge has been standing on the plain for thousands of years.

Pyramids - stand - desert - thousands

Visitors - come - Pyramids - hundreds

Tourists - visit - Statue of Liberty - many

People - sail - the Nile - thousands

1 Make sentences.

wear hunt catch live draw cook

on the walls fish skins and furs in caves wild animals over fires

Early people used to ______________________________.

They ______________________________.

______________________________.

______________________________.

______________________________.

______________________________.

2 Write questions about early people. Then write short answers.

Did they ______________________________? Yes, they did ______________.

______________________________ ______________.

______________________________ ______________.

______________________________ ______________.

______________________________ ______________.

3 Write sentences.

They did not ______________________________.

______________________________.

______________________________.

1 **Write the verbs.**

Choose from: think be live tell come look say sail

Thor Heyerdahl __________ from Norway. He __________ on islands in the Pacific for many years. He __________ that the islanders __________ there from South America a long time ago. Their statues __________ the same and they __________ the same stories. Many people __________ that Heyerdahl __________ wrong.

2 **Which is different?**

Norway	Peru	England	the Pacific	__________
branch	leaf	nest	trunk	__________
sledge	raft	yacht	rowing boat	__________
sailor	statue	fisherman	hunter	__________
ocean	island	lake	river	__________

Can you say why?

__________ is different because __________.

__________.

__________.

__________.

__________.

1 **Put these phrases in the right order and make a poem.**

His sword shines, too.

His uniform is always smart

How long have they been waiting there so quiet and still?

The soldier and his horse do not move.

Does he see the people there

and his boots always shine.

He holds it up in his right hand.

and looks along the busy street.

who are hurrying to work?

____

The soldier sits on his horse ______________________

____

____

____

____

____

For more than a hundred years. ______________________

2 **Can you think of a title for the poem?**

Dictionary skills

1 **Abbreviations.**

A dictionary gives you a list of abbreviations.

Match these abbreviations to words.

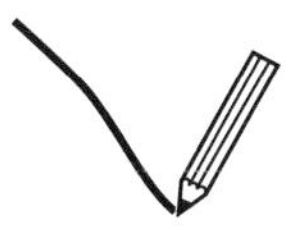

a.m.	Street
Aug.	for example
km	North
e.g.	August
Fri.	page
N.	in the morning
p.	the United States of America
p.m.	kilometres
St.	Friday
USA	in the afternoon

2 **Write.**

N. London	______________________	King St.	______________________
Fri. 2nd Aug.	______________________	at 4 p.m.	______________________
p. 62	______________________	100 km	______________________

Composition

1 **Here is the beginning and the end of a story. Can you write the part in the middle?**

Mark and Paul were on holiday. One day they went to play on the beach. There was a lot of wood on the beach so the two boys made a small raft. 'Let's sail the raft to that little island,' said Mark.

At last the two boys arrived back at their house. They were tired and wet and hungry. It had been a very exciting day but they were glad to be home.

20

1 Finish the sentences.

On the surface of the earth	it is very hot.
Deep in the earth	through these openings.
It is so hot	when it gets cold.
Sometimes there are openings	that the rocks are liquid.
Magma erupts	rocks are hard and solid.
Lava becomes solid	in rocks on the surface.

2 What are the words?

Lava is liquid when it is hot but ________________ when it is cold.

A volcano is a kind of ________________ .

When a volcano erupts, ________________ go up into the air.

Liquid lava is very ________________ .

There is magma under the ________________ of the earth.

Clouds of dust are ________________ into the air when a volcano erupts.

3 Fit the words above into the volcano.

1 Read this magazine report about Surtsey.
How many mistakes can you find? Underline them.

Have you heard of Surtsey? Surtsey is a mountain which suddenly appeared out of the sea near Norway about forty years ago. It was made by a volcano which erupted under the water. The rocks of Surtsey are made of lava.

The first people to see Surtsey were some tourists on a boat. They saw smoke and thought that it was coming from a burning house. When they went closer, they saw lava, dust and fire coming out of the sea. They stayed to watch because it was not dangerous.

Today plants grow on the island and lots of people live there.

Correct the mistakes.

______________________________.

______________________________.

______________________________.

______________________________.

______________________________.

______________________________.

2 Find the opposites.
Draw lines.

dangerous thin

rise liquid

heats hard

safe quickly

fall thick

noisily cools

solid quietly

soft slowly

Dictionary skills

1 **Match.**

volcano

sledge

raft

island

statue

cart

kilt

ring

well

calculator

2 **Write in ABC order.**

____

____

____

____

____

____

____

____

____

____

3 **Spelling.**
Add the missing letters.

ba ___ ___

___ ___ ips

la ___ ___

bru ___ ___

___ ___ eel

___ ___ oon

swi ___ ___

___ ___ ince

___ ___ idge

ma ___ ___

cha ___ ___

___ ___ ant

Composition

1 **The summer holidays are nearly here.**

Can you remember your holiday last year?
Where did you go?
What did you see?
What did you do?
Who did you meet?
Did you have a good time?

What about this year?
Where are you going?
Who will you go with?
What are you going to do?
What are you hoping to see?
Are you going to have fun?

Write about your holiday last year and this year. And draw a picture!

Last year ... this year ...

Revision

1 **Write the verbs.**
Past or past perfect?

The people of Pompeii ____________________ about the volcano because

it ____________________ quiet for hundreds of years. (not worry; be)

Some people ________________________ that the water in their

wells ___________________________________ . (notice; disappear)

After the volcano ____________________ , no-one ____________________
live in the town. (erupt; can)

In 1860 workmen ____________________ to move the rock which

____________________ the town for nearly 2000 years. (start; cover)

2 **Write the sentences.**

She said that ____ .

____ .

____ .

She told Marcus that ____ .

____ .

3 **Write the sentences.**

She told Marcus ____ .

____ .

____ .

She asked Marcus ____ .

____ .

4 Write the verbs. Present or future?

If you ______________ to Pompeii, you ______________ mosaics. (go; see)

I ______________ you when I ______________ home. (phone; get)

John ______________ late if he ______________ up. (be; not hurry)

When you ______________ my house, you ______________ my parents. (visit; meet)

5 Finish the sentences.

If he had enough money, Henry ______________________________ .

If he went there, he ______________________________ .

Sally would be happy if ______________________________ .

If she had enough time, ______________________________ .

Mike would get thinner if ______________________________ .

6 Write the sentences.

Like this: cows - milk - farmer's wife — *The cows are milked by the farmer's wife.*

cotton - grow - hot countries ______________________________ .

jeans - make - cotton cloth ______________________________ .

paper - invent - Chinese ______________________________ .

dam - build - 1946 ______________________________ .

tombs - find - travellers ______________________________ .

My English Scrapbook

English writing is everywhere! Collect labels, adverts and signs in English.

My English Scrapbook

Who do you know who speaks English? Collect pictures.

actors   singers   people in history

cartoon characters   actresses

teachers people in books politicians

famous people scientists

My English Scrapbook

Where is English spoken? Label the countries and collect pictures of them.

England America Australia

New Zealand South Africa

Canada Kenya Zambia

Nigeria India Pakistan

My English Scrapbook

What is your favourite song or poem in English? Write it here.